Jayne Netley Mayhew's
CROSS
STITCH
Animal
COLLECTION

Jayne Netley Mayhew's
CROSS STITCH
Animal COLLECTION

David & Charles

For Ian, Biggles and Felix with love

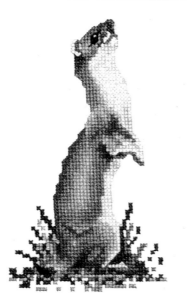

A DAVID & CHARLES BOOK

First published in the UK in 2002
Reprinted 2002, 2003
First paperback edition 2004

Distributed in North America
by F&W Publications, Inc.
4700 East Galbraith Road
Cincinnati, OH 45236
1-800-289-0963

A catalogue record for this book is available from the British Library.

ISBN 0 7153 1132 8 hardback
ISBN 0 7153 2031 9 paperback

Printed in Italy by Canale
for David & Charles
Brunel House   Newton Abbot   Devon

Executive editor   Cheryl Brown
Art editor   Ali Myer
Project editor   Linda Clements
Book designer   Lisa Forrester
Photographer   Jon Bouchier

Visit our website at www.davidandcharles.co.uk

David & Charles books are available from all good bookshops;
alternatively you can contact our Orderline on (0)1626 334555
or write to us at FREEPOST EX2110, David & Charles Direct,
Newton Abbot, TQ12 4ZZ (no stamp required UK mainland).

CONTENTS

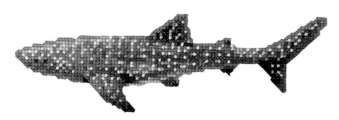

INTRODUCTION

THIS IS MY FIFTH EMBROIDERY BOOK, which has been a real pleasure to work on as it has allowed me to bring the pages alive with many of my favourite animals. There are five themed collections, each reflecting a distinctive world habitat. The projects begin with the Safari Collection, with lions and their prey on the dusty plains of Africa. From here you are launched skyward with some of the spectacular birds that are Masters of the Air, then back to earth with Forest Creatures amid their leafy woodlands. The depths of the seas are then plumbed in Ocean Life, where you can seek out some of the fascinating inhabitants. Finally the frozen wastes of the globe are explored with a detailed look at Polar Wildlife.

Each chapter begins with a superb collage-type design, filled with a selection of creatures that inhabit that particular environment. This is followed by three additional designs, all providing a detailed picture of animal life. I have tried throughout the book to provide a wide variety of subjects to stitch – from a pair of foxes with their distinctive red coats to more unusual subjects like the jellyfish, which are stitched using only one strand of stranded cotton (floss) to make them look delicate and translucent.

The designs are suitable for stitchers of all abilities. The rhinoceros and the puma for example, although detailed and realistic portraits, are stitched using just whole cross stitch. For the more experienced stitchers there are several enjoyable challenges, like the Tawny Owl and the Little Bee-eaters, where the use of French knots and backstitch are added for extra finishing detail to the designs.

Each project has instructions for stitching, the fabric and threads you will need and is illustrated with a large colour photograph and a full-colour chart. Each chapter is completed by a Display It page, where I suggest many ideas on how to stitch and use the designs. The projects use a variety of simple stitches including cross stitch, three-quarter cross stitch, backstitch,

French knots and long stitch. These are all described at the back of the book in the Workbox chapter, which also gives you useful advice on the materials and equipment you will need, basic stitching techniques and the many ways the projects in the book can be displayed and made up.

I hope stitchers of all levels and abilities will find this book an inspiration. Not only is it crammed with fascinating and realistically portrayed animals, it also provides ideas on how to alter and adapt designs, how to change fabrics and threads, and how to alter stitches to give a whole new look to a design. Cross stitch is such an attractive and versatile stitch – all you need is a little inspiration to go with it. I wish you many, many hours of happy stitching.

Jayne Netley Mayhew.

SAFARI
COLLECTION

REFLECTING THE WARM COLOURS of the savannah, this design includes some of my favourite African animals. In the centre is the queen of the beasts, a beautiful, alert lioness framed by grasses. I was spoilt for choice when it came to choosing designs to surround her with as so many came to mind. Finally I decided on a family scene and a solitary male lion resting in the sun. Another well-known African animal and the largest, the elephant, was a definite choice. I also included two other distinctive African animals — a zebra with its attractive striped colouring and an elegant male impala head. The whole design makes a wonderfully impressive framed picture but each of the motifs works equally well stitched up on its own — see page 11, and the suggestions in Display It, page 28.

Following this main piece are three additional designs. There are cute ring-tailed lemurs from Madagascar, a young springbok perfectly at home in the grasslands, and to finish the collection, an impressive rhinoceros head.

Safari Collection

STITCH IT

Fabric: 28 count sand Zweigart Brittney
59 x 59cm (23 x 23in)

Threads: DMC stranded cotton (floss)

Stitch count: 209 x 209

Design size: 38 x 38cm
(15 x 15in) approximately

Stitches: Whole cross stitch,
three-quarter cross stitch,
backstitch, long stitch

Prepare your fabric for work and mark the centre point (see Workbox). Follow the chart on pages 12–15, using two strands of stranded cotton (floss) for all cross stitch and working over two threads of evenweave fabric.

Work the backstitch with two strands of 310 for the details on the zebra, lioness, cubs and impala. Work the backstitch on the elephant with one strand of 648. Work the long stitches for the lioness' whiskers and eyebrows in one strand of white (shown in black on the chart for clarity).

To complete, mount and frame your picture or see Display It, page 28.

SAFARI COLLECTION THREAD LIST

1 skein each DMC stranded cotton (floss)

310	black	433	med brown golden	356	med terracotta	840	med beige brown
975	v. dk rust	3772	v. dk desert sand	831	med golden olive	648	lt beaver grey
blanc	white	434	lt brown golden	780	ultra v. dk topaz	839	dk beige brown
400	dk mahogany	3787	dk brown grey	829	v. dk golden olive	3072	v. lt beaver grey
3371	black brown	435	v. lt brown golden	781	v. dk topaz	3827	v. lt rust
300	v. dk mahogany	3022	med brown grey	844	ultra dk beaver grey	422	lt hazelnut brown
938	ultra dk coffee brown	738	v. lt tan	543	ultra v. lt beige brown	977	lt rust
945	tawny	3023	lt brown grey	645	v. dk beaver grey	3828	hazelnut brown
898	v. dk coffee brown	739	ultra v. lt tan	842	v. lt beige brown	976	med rust
951	lt tawny	3024	v. lt brown grey	646	dk beaver grey	420	dk hazelnut brown
801	dk coffee brown	712	cream	841	lt beige brown	3826	dk rust
3770	v. lt tawny	833	lt golden olive	647	med beaver grey	869	v. dk hazelnut brown

2 skeins each DMC stranded cotton (floss)

436	tan	437	lt tan

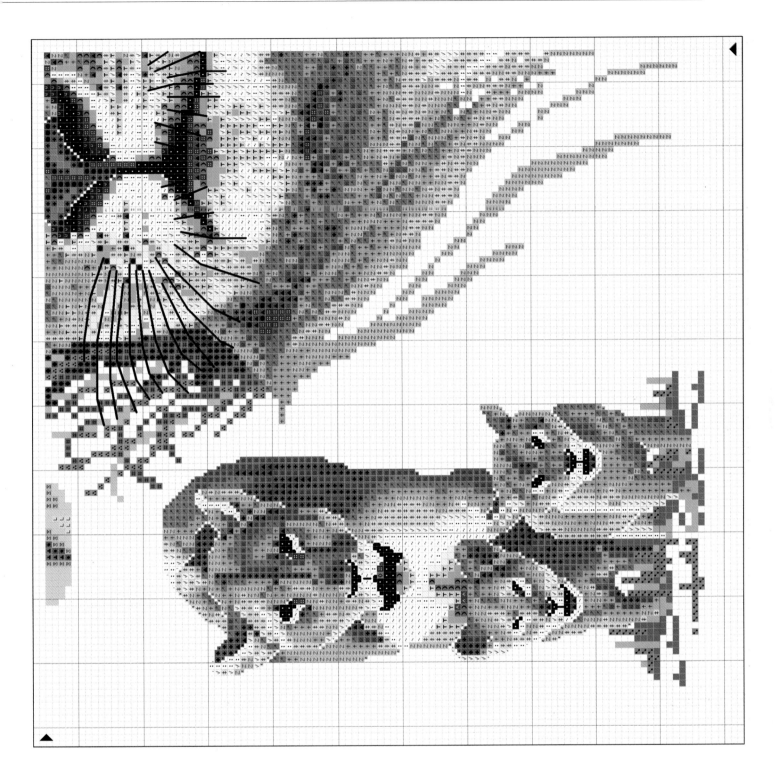

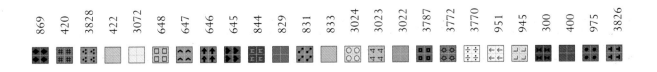

869 420 3828 422 3072 648 647 646 645 844 829 831 833 3024 3023 3022 3787 3772 3770 951 945 300 400 975 3826

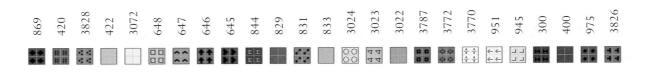

Ring-tailed Lemurs

ONE OF MY FAVOURITE ANIMALS is the ring-tailed lemur from Madagascar as they look like little bandits with their banded tails, bright eyes and pointy faces. As much at home on the ground as in the trees, they are a familiar sight strolling along in a group, their tails held high like banners. They rest, sleep and groom in groups, keeping warm with their tails wrapped around them. It is difficult to tell how many there are until the heads pop out.

The word lemur means ghost, as some lemurs have weird-sounding calls. The ring-tailed is sometimes called the cat lemur, as one of its calls sounds like the meow of a cat.

STITCH IT

Fabric: 14 count cream Aida, 54 x 41cm (21 x 16in)

Threads: DMC stranded cotton (floss) (see thread list page 27)

Stitch count: 180 x 110

Design size: 33 x 21cm (13 x 8in) approx

Stitches: Whole cross stitch, French knots

Prepare your fabric for work and mark the centre point (see Workbox). Follow the chart on pages 18/19, using two strands of stranded cotton (floss) for all cross stitch. Work the French knots in two strands of white for the eye highlights.

Mount and frame your picture to complete or see Display It, page 28.

	3047
	3046
4 4 / 4 4	524
	523
	522
	520
✓ ✓ / ✓ ✓	3024
	3023
	3022
m m / m m	3787
	3021
‖ ‖ / ‖ ‖	976
	3826
	975
	300
	613
	3864
# # / # #	3863
	3862
L L / L L	3033
	3782
7 7 / 7 7	3032
: : / : :	712
↑ ↑ / ↑ ↑	543
T T / T T	842
	841
	840
	801
	938
U U / U U	3371
	415
	414
	317
	413
H H / H H	3799
~ ~ / ~ ~	white
	310

RING-TAILED LEMURS KEY

Springbok

THIS YOUNG SPRINGBOK is just like a foal, all legs and wide-eyed. They are dependent on their mothers for six months, their sand-coloured coats helping to camouflage them on the South African plains. The springbok gets its name from its response to danger – when alarmed, it drops its head, arches its back and springs stiff-legged into the air up to two metres. At the same time a dorsal pouch lined with long white hairs is everted, displaying a prominent crest. Springbok were once numbered in millions, but were slaughtered wholesale when they came into competition with domestic animals. In recent years though they have been recovering in numbers.

STITCH IT

Fabric:	*14 count cream Aida, 43 x 44cm (17 x 17¼in)*
Threads:	*DMC stranded cotton (floss) (see thread list page 27)*
Stitch count:	*125 x 130*
Design size:	*23 x 24cm (9 x 9¼in) approx*
Stitches:	*Whole cross stitch, three-quarter cross stitch, backstitch*

Prepare your fabric for work and mark the centre point (see Workbox). Follow the chart on pages 22/23, using two strands of stranded cotton (floss) for all cross stitch. Work the backstitch in one strand of 310 for the eye and mouth details.

Mount and frame your picture to complete or see Display It, page 28.

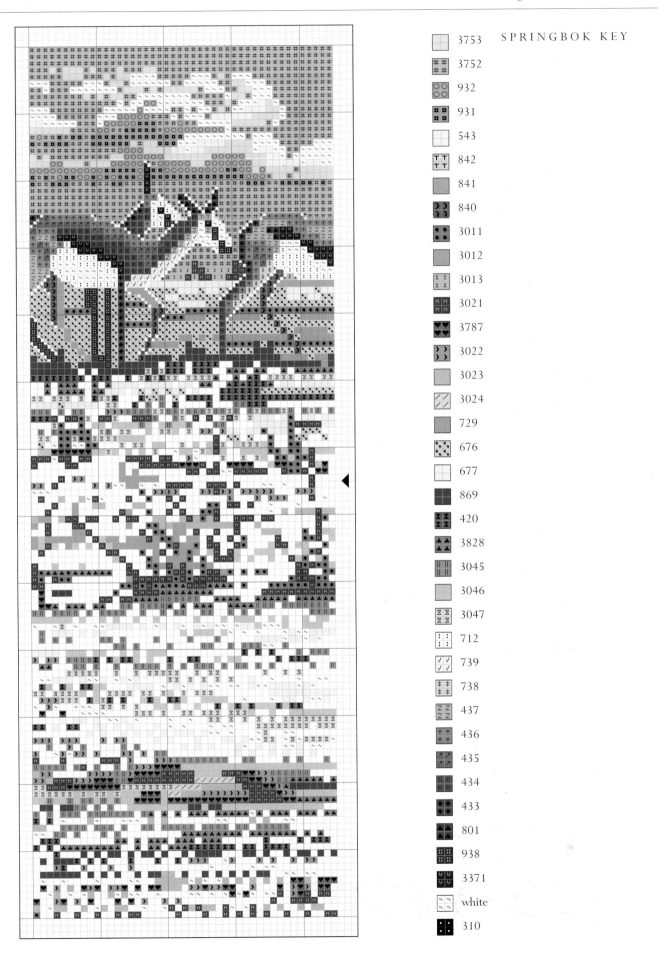

SPRINGBOK KEY

▦	3753
⊞	3752
⊚	932
⊡	931
▢	543
T T	842
▨	841
❭❭	840
••	3011
▩	3012
I I	3013
H H	3021
♥♥	3787
❭❭	3022
▢	3023
⁄⁄	3024
▨	729
⋰⋰	676
▢	677
■	869
✕✕	420
♣♣	3828
‖‖	3045
▨	3046
Σ Σ	3047
⋮⋮	712
√ √	739
‡ ‡	738
Z Z	437
+ +	436
▨	435
▨	434
✚✚	433
▲▲	801
▦	938
U U	3371
~ ~	white
■	310

Rhinoceros

AFTER THE ELEPHANT, the rhinoceros is the second largest African animal. It can weigh 2,000kg and has a reputation not to be taken lightly. Its tendency to aggressive and bad-tempered over-reaction is caused in part to extreme short-sightedness, though it does have acute senses of smell and hearing. Africa has two rhinos, the black and the white – both grey in colour. They have two long horns but their skin is much less folded than other rhinos and they lack front teeth. The white rhino feeds entirely on grass, while the rarer black rhino is a browser. This design is easy to stitch as it has only whole cross stitch. It uses various shades of greys and browns to give the impression of a dusty, muddy hide.

STITCH IT

Fabric:	*14 count cream Aida 38 x 43cm (15 x 17in)*
Threads:	*DMC stranded cotton (floss) (see thread list page 27)*
Stitch count:	*100 x 126*
Design size:	*18 x 23cm (7 x 9in) approx*
Stitches:	*Whole cross stitch*

Prepare your fabric for work and mark the centre point (see Workbox). Follow the chart on page 26, using two strands of stranded cotton (floss) for all the cross stitches.

Mount and frame your picture to complete or see Display It, page 28.

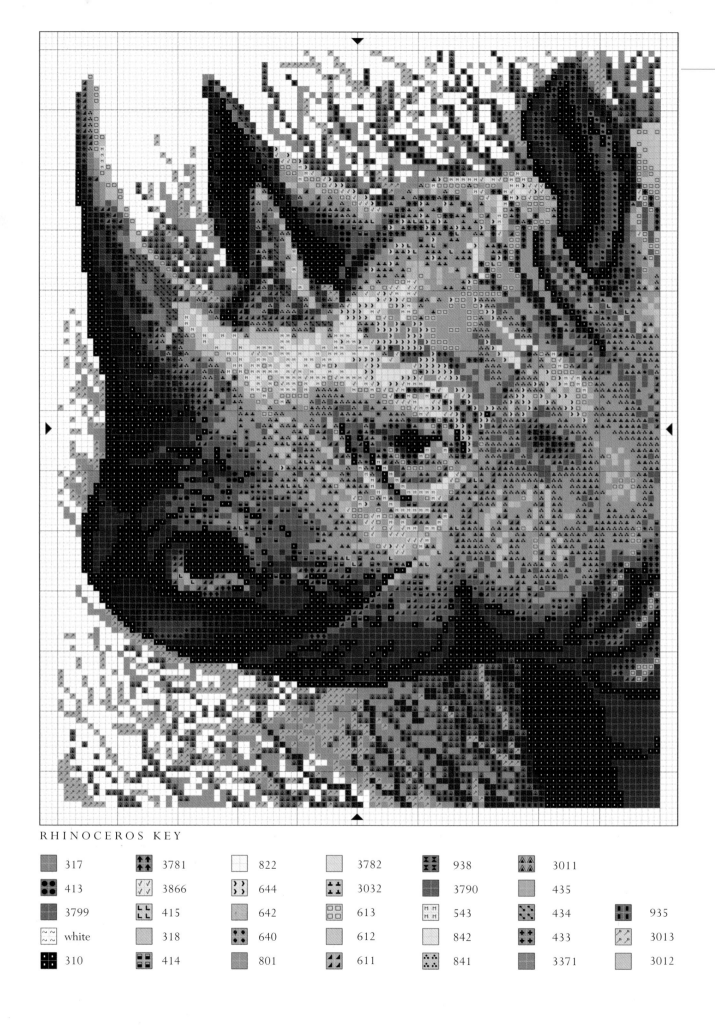

RHINOCEROS KEY

317	3781	822	3782	938	3011
413	3866	644	3032	3790	435
3799	415	642	613	543	434	935
white	318	640	612	842	433	3013
310	414	801	611	841	3371	3012

RING-TAILED LEMURS THREAD LIST
1 skein each DMC stranded cotton (floss)

310	black	414	dk silver grey	840	med beige brown	3032	med mocha brown
3863	med brown	3826	dk rust	3023	lt brown grey	524	v. lt fern green
blanc	white	415	silver grey	841	lt beige brown	3782	lt mocha brown
3864	lt brown	976	med rust	3024	v. lt brown grey	3046	med yellow beige
3799	v. dk pewter grey	3371	black brown	842	v. lt beige brown	3033	v. lt mocha brown
613	v. lt drab brown	3021	v. dk brown grey	520	dk fern green	3047	lt yellow beige
413	dk silver grey	938	ultra dk coffee brown	543	ultra v. lt beige brown	3862	dk brown
300	v. dk mahogany	3787	dk brown grey	522	fern green		
317	silver grey	801	dk coffee brown	712	cream		
975	v. dk rust	3022	med brown grey	523	lt fern green		

Brock, Scarlet

12/14/2022

Item(s) Checked Out

TITLE   Bounty Hunter
BARCODE   33029108444712
DUE DATE   12-27-22

Total Items This Session: 1

You saved $129.95 by visiting the library today!

Books are just the beginning.

Use your library card to access ebooks, audiobooks, and magazines. Plus, you can check out Wi-Fi hotspots and Chromebooks, learn a new language and get free museum passes.

Terminal #   12

golden	738	v. lt tan	3045	dk yellow beige
grey	3011	dk khaki green	931	med antique blue
den	739	ultra v. lt tan	3828	hazelnut brown
ey	840	med beige brown	932	lt antique blue
olden	712	cream	420	dk hazelnut brown
grey	841	lt beige brown	3752	v. lt antique blue
	3047	lt yellow beige	869	v. dk hazelnut brown
	842	v. lt beige brown	3753	ultra v. lt antique blue
	3046	med yellow beige		
een	543	ultra v. lt beige brown		

y	801	dk coffee brown	611	drab brown
e brown	434	lt brown golden	935	dk avocado green
	640	v. dk beige grey	612	lt drab brown
ge grey	435	v. lt brown golden		
	642	dk beige grey		
fee brown	3011	dk khaki green		
	644	med beige grey		
h	3012	med khaki green		
rown	822	lt beige grey		
golden	3013	lt khaki green		

DISPLAY IT

The designs in this section are wonderfully
adaptable for use on all sorts of items and can be
displayed in various ways. For example, you could
inset the male lion motif into a mug, stitching it on
a smaller count fabric such as an 18 count. Special
mugs are available from companies like Framecraft
(see Suppliers). The female lion head would make a
wonderful central image on a cushion, either on a
sand-coloured Aida or linen, or perhaps on a
contrasting blue or khaki colour. You could also use
waste canvas to stitch designs on clothing, such as
on the two smock tops shown here (see page 119
for details on using waste canvas). One smock top
is adorned with the elephant motif from the main
Safari Collection collage, while the other features
the zebra. You could stitch the designs on a wide
variety of clothing, such as sweat-shirts, blouses and
babies' bibs.

MASTERS OF THE AIR

A FABULOUS AERIAL DISPLAY opens this section, with a collection of some of my favourite birds of prey amid a cloud-covered, mountainous region. Overlooking all with a steely gaze is a magnificent golden eagle. Around him are images of a snowy owl, an eagle in flight, a hovering kestrel, two delightful tawny owl chicks and a bald eagle. I particularly enjoyed depicting the distinctive plumage of the snowy owl and the fierce eyes of the bald eagle. I included the kestrel as it is a familiar sight near my home. The collage would be most impressive stitched as a single piece or you could work the motifs singly, see page 33.

Following this main piece there are three additional designs – all masters of the air in their own way. There is a wonderfully detailed tawny owl, alert on a tree stump for a glimpse of prey. This is followed by a truly delightful study of a branch full of little bee-eaters, their emerald and orange plumage vividly depicted. Finally, there are flight portraits of blue tits and robins, showing their distinctive plumage.

Masters of the Air

STITCH IT

Fabric:	*28 count ice blue Zweigart Brittney 59 x 59cm (23 x 23in)*
Threads:	*DMC stranded cotton (floss)*
Stitch count:	*209 x 209*
Design size:	*38 x 38cm (15 x 15in) approximately*
Stitches:	*Whole cross stitch, three-quarter cross stitch, backstitch, French knots*

Prepare your fabric for work and mark the centre point (see Workbox). Follow the chart on pages 34–37, using two strands of stranded cotton (floss) for all cross stitch, worked over two threads of evenweave fabric.

Work the backstitches using one strand. Black 310 for the golden eagle's eye and beak, kestrel's wing, tail, breast and back feathers, snowy owl's eye and beak, the bald eagle's eyes, and the tawny owl chicks' eyes. Use 726 for the kestrel's eye and 841 for the bald eagle's beak. Work the French knots in one strand of white for the snowy owl and bald eagle eye highlights.

Mount and frame your picture to complete or see Display It, page 46.

MASTERS OF THE AIR THREAD LIST

1 skein each DMC stranded cotton (floss)

3371	black brown	3023	lt brown grey	318	lt silver grey	937	med avocado green
453	lt shell grey	977	lt rust	3768	dk grey green	920	med red copper
938	ultra dk coffee brown	3024	v. lt brown grey	415	silver grey	469	avocado green
452	med shell grey	3827	v. lt rust	3823	ultra pale yellow	921	copper
801	dk coffee brown	3051	dk green grey	762	v. lt pearl grey	470	lt avocado green
451	dk shell grey	3799	v. dk pewter grey	3042	lt silver plum	840	med beige brown
300	v. dk mahogany	3052	med green grey	725	topaz	436	tan
535	v. lt ash grey	413	dk silver grey	543	ultra v. lt beige brown	727	v. lt topaz
975	v. dk rust	928	v. lt grey green	726	lt topaz	437	lt tan
3787	dk brown grey	317	silver grey	742	lt tangerine	842	v. lt beige brown
3826	dk rust	927	lt grey green	3078	v. lt golden yellow	738	v. lt tan
3022	med brown grey	414	dk silver grey	934	black avocado green	841	lt beige brown
976	med rust	926	med grey green	919	red copper	739	ultra v. lt tan

2 skeins each DMC stranded cotton (floss)

310	black

3 skeins each DMC stranded cotton (floss)

blanc	white

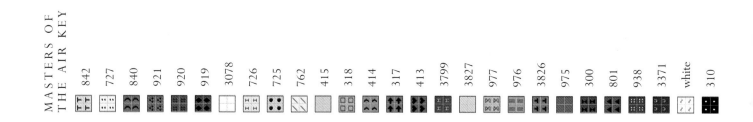

842 727 840 921 920 919 3078 726 725 762 415 318 414 317 413 3799 3827 977 976 3826 975 300 801 938 3371 white 310

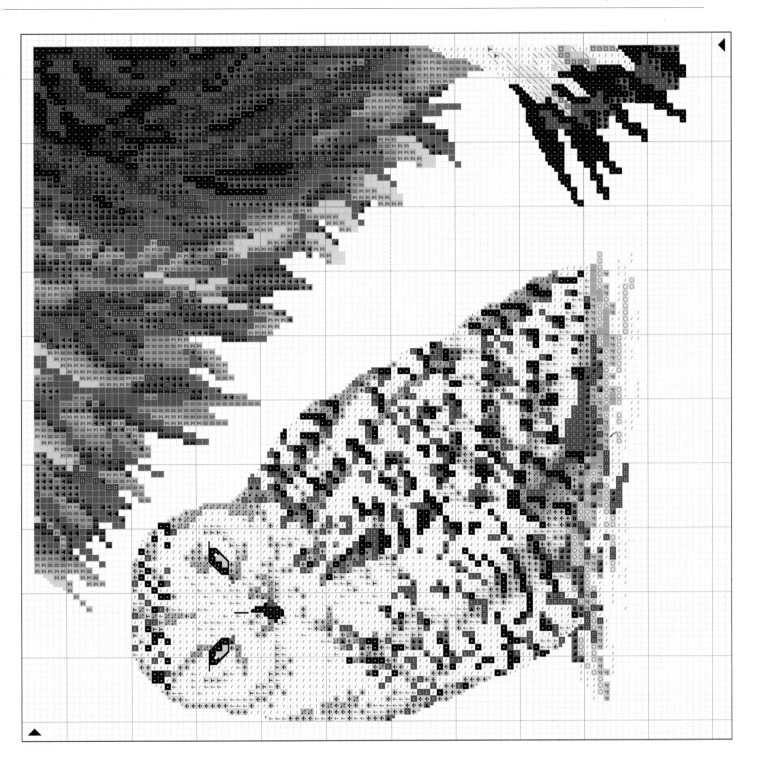

739 738 437 436 470 469 937 934 742 543 3042 3823 3768 926 927 928 3052 3051 3024 3023 3022 3787 535 451 452 453 841

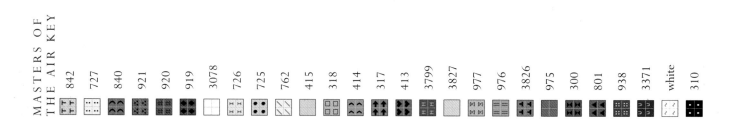

842 · 727 · 840 · 921 · 920 · 919 · 3078 · 726 · 725 · 762 · 415 · 318 · 414 · 317 · 413 · 3799 · 3827 · 977 · 976 · 3826 · 975 · 300 · 801 · 938 · 3371 · white · 310

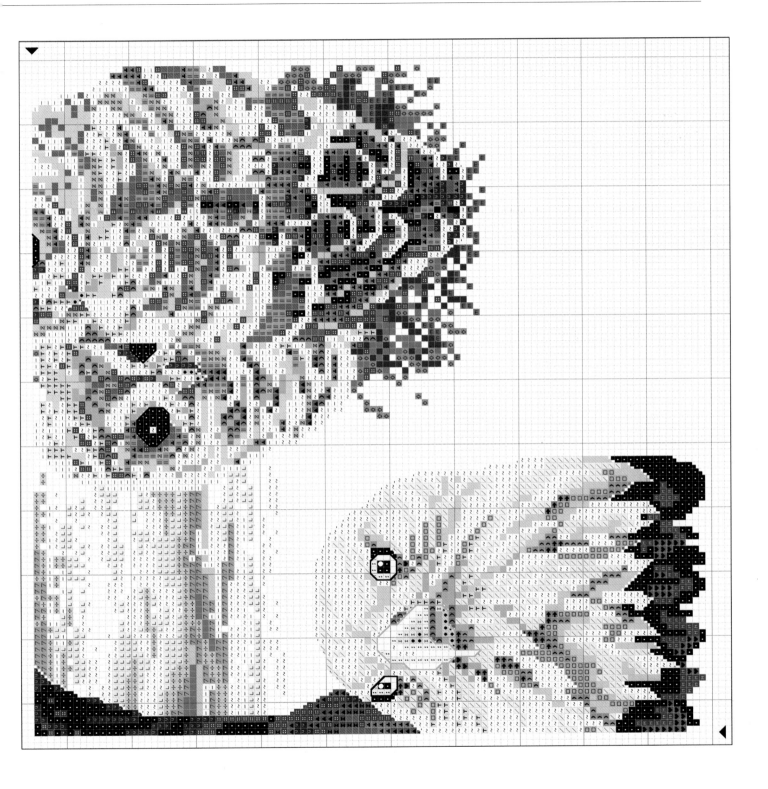

Tawny Owl

THIS IS ONE OF MY FAVOURITE OWLS, shown here perched on a tree stump covered in sulphur tuft toadstools, lichen and moss. The owl is nocturnal and can hunt in complete darkness, using only its superb hearing to locate its prey. They figure frequently in tales of witchcraft and the supernatural and were thought to have the gift of prophecy and unusual intelligence. The owl is pictured here stitched on black, with a mixture of French knots and backstitch used to give greater detail to the moss and lichen. It would look equally good stitched on sage green or sky blue.

STITCH IT

Fabric:	14 count black Aida 41 x 47cm (16 x 18½in)
Threads:	DMC stranded cotton (floss)
Stitch count:	109 x 144
Design size:	21 x 27cm (8 x 10½in) approx
Stitches:	Whole cross stitch, three-quarter cross stitch, backstitch, French knots

Prepare your fabric for work and mark the centre point (see Workbox). Follow the chart on pages 40/41, using two strands of stranded cotton (floss) for all cross stitch. For the lichen and moss details work backstitches and French knots, using one strand of 524 and 921. Use 310 black for the backstitch around the owl's eyes.

Mount and frame your picture to complete or see Display It, page 46.

TAWNY OWL THREAD LIST
1 skein each DMC stranded cotton (floss)

310	black	3346	dk yellow green	677	v. lt golden sand	611	drab brown
3051	dk green grey	3826	dk rust	934	black avocado green	3790	ultra dk beige grey
blanc	white	3347	med yellow green	746	off white	612	lt drab brown
3052	med green grey	976	med rust	936	v. dk avocado green	640	v. dk beige grey
3371	black brown	3829	v. dk golden sand	840	med beige brown	613	v. lt drab brown
3053	green grey	977	lt rust	469	avocado green	642	dk beige grey
938	ultra dk coffee brown	680	dk golden sand	841	lt beige brown	918	dk red copper
524	v. lt fern green	3827	v. lt rust	470	lt avocado green	644	med beige grey
801	dk coffee brown	3820	dk straw	842	v. lt beige brown	920	med copper
895	v. dk hunter green	945	tawny	471	v. lt avocado green	822	lt beige grey
300	v. dk mahogany	3821	med straw	3799	v. dk pewter grey	921	copper
3345	v. dk yellow green	676	lt golden sand	610	dk drab brown		
975	v. dk rust	3822	lt straw	413	dk silver grey		

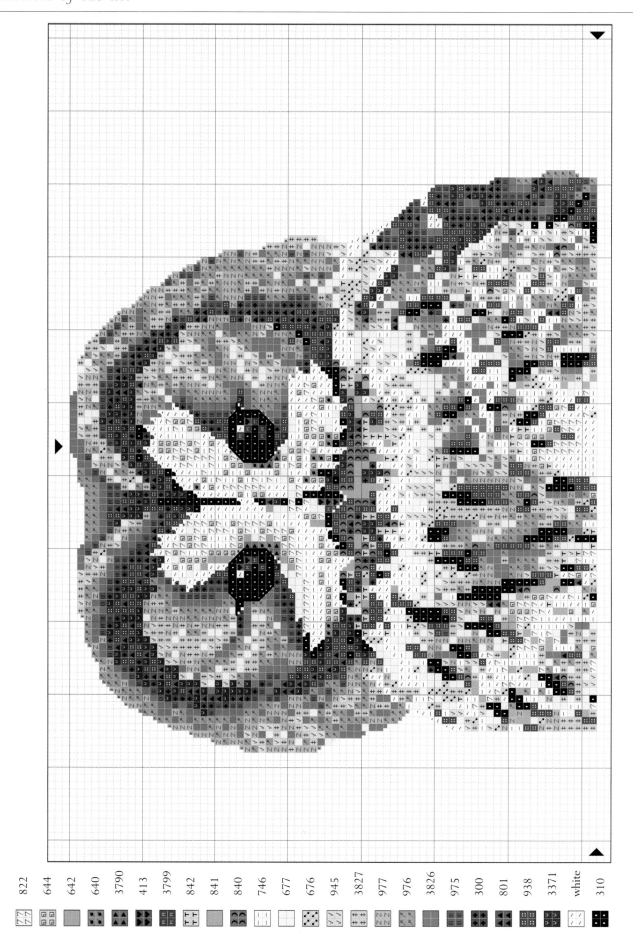

TAWNY OWL KEY

822 644 642 640 3790 413 3799 842 841 840 746 677 676 945 3827 977 976 3826 975 300 801 938 3371 white 310

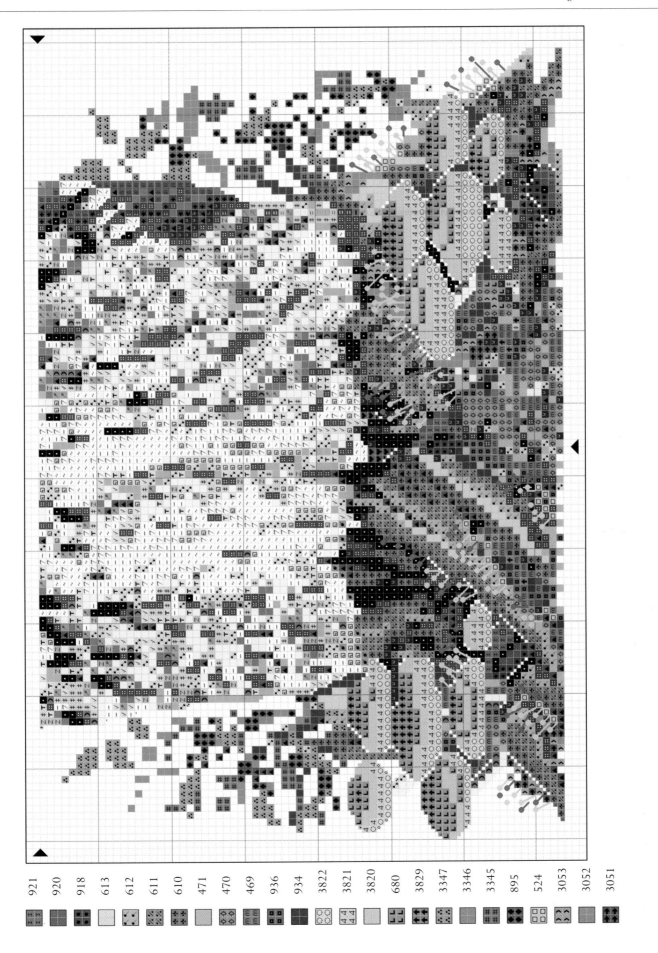

921 920 918 613 612 611 610 471 470 469 936 934 3822 3821 3820 680 3829 3347 3346 3345 895 524 3053 3052 3051

Little Bee-eaters

THESE BEAUTIFUL, JEWEL-LIKE BIRDS are one of the most abundant of the African bee-eaters. A common bird in open country with bushes and scattered trees, they are the smallest of the bee-eaters, measuring on average a length of 16cm (6in). They are generally found in pairs or small family groups. In my design I have shown an endearing family group, huddled on a reed stem. As usual when you see a family group, there is always one odd bird sitting in the opposite direction. Do they do this for a reason, so he can watch their backs, or does he just want to be different?

STITCH IT

Fabric:	*14 count ecru Aida*
	48 x 41cm (19 x 16in)
Threads:	*DMC stranded cotton (floss)*
	(see thread list page 49)
Stitch count:	*155 x 109*
Design size:	*28 x 21cm (11 x 8in) approx*
Stitches:	*Whole cross stitch, three-quarter*
	cross stitch, backstitch, French knots

Prepare your fabric for work and mark the centre point (see Workbox). Follow the chart on pages 44/45, using two strands of stranded cotton (floss) for all cross stitch. Work the backstitch in one strand, using 310 black around the eyes, 453 around the beaks and 951 for the tail and wing feathers. Work the French knots for the grass seed-heads using two strands of 676 and use one strand of white for the eye highlights.

Mount and frame your picture to complete or see Display It, page 46.

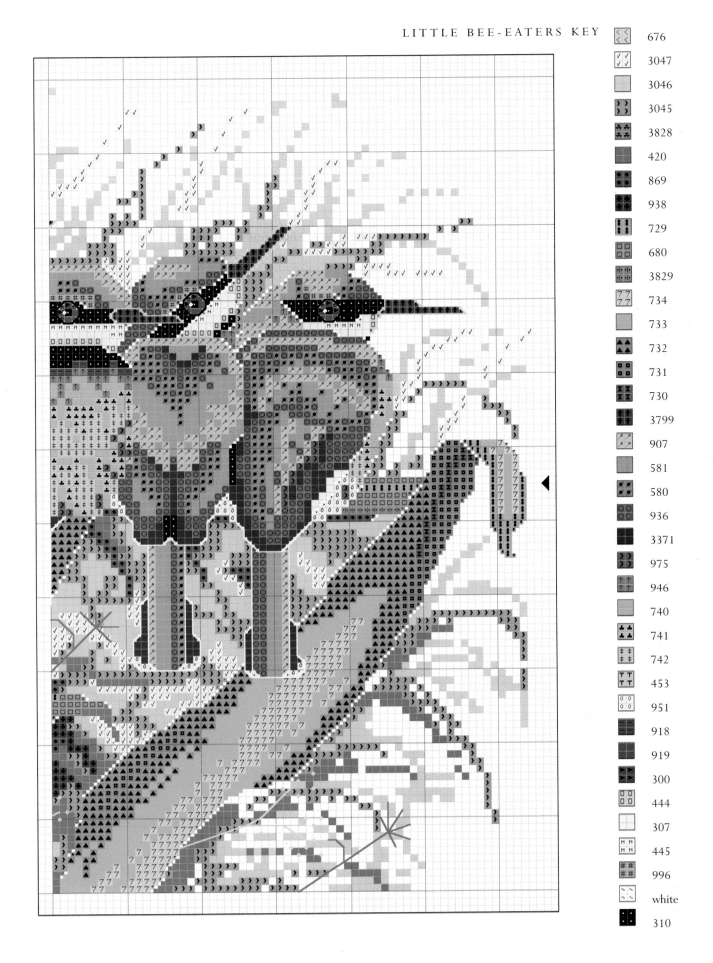

	676
	3047
	3046
	3045
	3828
	420
	869
	938
	729
	680
	3829
	734
	733
	732
	731
	730
	3799
	907
	581
	580
	936
	3371
	975
	946
	740
	741
	742
	453
	951
	918
	919
	300
	444
	307
	445
	996
	white
	310

Robin and Blue Tit

TWO OF THE MOST CHARMING garden visitors are the robin and blue tit. The robin's friendliness towards gardeners is renowned and the little bird is frequently associated with Christmas. The blue tit is a well-known visitor to anyone who has a peanut feeder in their garden. This acrobatic little bird is a great favourite of mine. In both of my designs they are shown in flight, wings outstretched. They work wonderfully as a mobile but there are any number of ways to use these lovely little designs.

STITCH IT

Fabric:	*14 count white Aida 23 x 23cm (9 x 9in)*
Threads:	*DMC stranded cotton (floss) (see thread list on page 49)*
Stitch count:	*Robin 49 x 63: Blue tit 39 x 61*
Design size:	*Robin 9 x 12cm (3½ x 4½in): Blue tit 7 x 11cm (2¾ x 4¼in)*
Stitches:	*Whole cross stitch, three-quarter cross stitch, backstitch, French knots*

Prepare your fabric for work and mark the centre point (see Workbox). Follow the chart on page 48, using two strands of stranded cotton (floss) for all cross stitch. Work all the backstitch using one strand – black 310 for the beaks and eyes and 413 for the wing and tail feathers. Work the French knots for the eye highlights in one strand of white.

The designs can be displayed as a plant stick or a mobile, or a single bird could be mounted as a picture. See also Display It, right.

To make up as a plant stick

You will need matching sewing thread and a thin stick. Take the two matching designs and stitch the two sides together, leaving a small gap in the stitching at the bottom of the body. Push a stick up though the gap and far enough in between the two layers for the embroidery to be held firmly in place.

To make up as a mobile

You will need a heavyweight interfacing, an iron, some white or invisible sewing thread and a hoop or branch. There are four birds on the mobile (eight designs in total). Start by placing the interfacing neatly over the embroidery, put a damp cloth over the designs and press with an iron. When the interfacing has bonded to both sides, trim the fabric to within 2.5cm (1in) of the design. Do not trim all the excess fabric at this stage. Now stitch the two sides together, sewing through both designs as close to the stitching as possible, with white or invisible sewing thread, matching up each side stitch by stitch. Trim away all the excess fabric, as close as possible to the stitching, to within one stitch from the edge of the design. String each embroidery with variable lengths of invisible thread and attach to a hoop or branch at intervals.

DISPLAY IT

The attractive designs in this section can be made up in a multitude of ways. For example, you could use a single robin or blue tit mounted into a teapot or

coffeepot stand. If stitched on a smaller count fabric, such as an 18 count, these birds could also be inset into mugs or cards. By using waste canvas many of the designs could be stitched on clothing. The beautiful little bee-eaters could be made up into a wonderful rectangular cushion, with a frilled or braided edge (see page 124 for instructions).

The tawny owl would make a wonderful doorstop, stitched up on a 10 count fabric to make him a little larger (see page 125 for instructions). Remember, if you alter the count, you will need different amounts of fabric and threads. On a 10 count I would use three strands of stranded cotton (floss); on an 18 count I would use one strand.

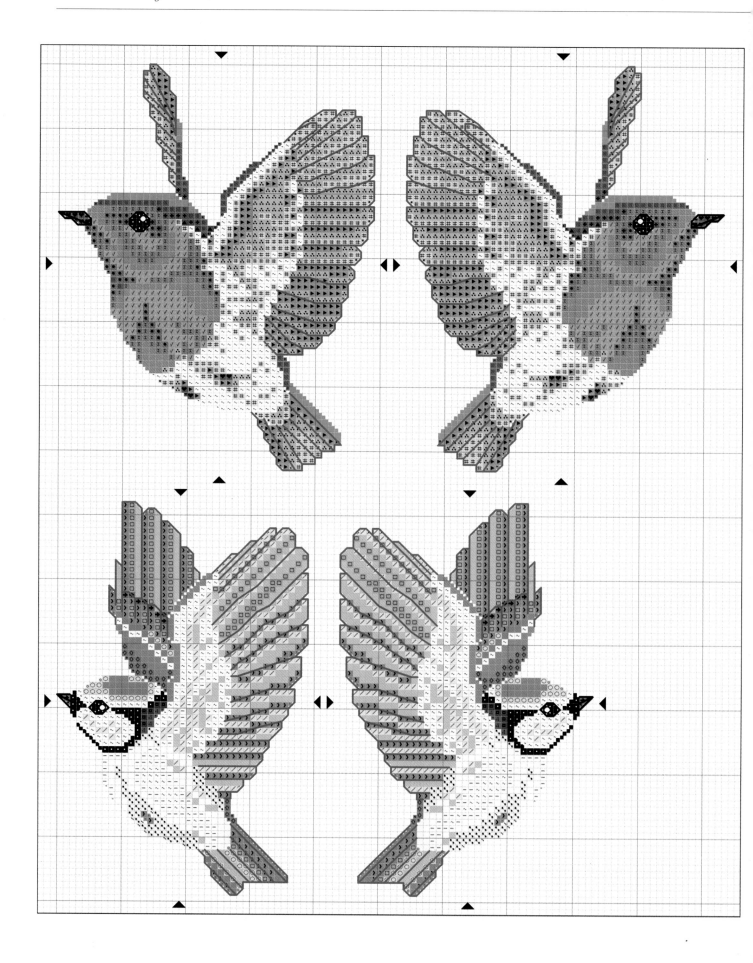

LITTLE BEE-EATERS THREAD LIST

1 skein each DMC stranded cotton (floss)

310	black	444	dk lemon	453	lt shell grey	975	v. dk rust
581	moss green	732	olive green	729	med golden sand	3045	dk yellow beige
blanc	white	300	v. dk mahogany	742	lt tangerine	3371	black brown
907	lt parrot green	733	med olive green	938	ultra dk coffee brown	3046	med yellow beige
996	med electric blue	919	red copper	741	med tangerine	936	v. dk avocado green
3799	v. dk pewter grey	734	lt olive green	869	v. dk hazelnut brown	3047	lt yellow beige
445	lt lemon	918	dk red copper	740	tangerine	580	dk moss green
730	v. dk olive green	3829	v. dk golden sand	420	dk hazelnut brown	676	lt golden sand
307	lemon	951	lt tawny	946	med burnt orange		
731	dk olive green	680	dk golden sand	3828	hazelnut brown		

ROBIN THREAD LIST

1 skein each DMC stranded cotton (floss)

310	black	801	dk coffee brown	434	lt brown golden	900	dk burnt orange
946	med burnt orange	970	lt pumpkin	648	lt beaver grey	413	dk silver grey
blanc	white	433	med brown golden	436	tan		
947	burnt orange	3072	v. lt beaver grey	647	med beaver grey		

BLUE TIT THREAD LIST

1 skein each DMC stranded cotton (floss)

310	black	762	v. lt pearl grey	311	med navy blue	413	dk silver grey
745	lt pale yellow	334	med baby blue	414	dk silver grey	3823	ultra pale yellow
blanc	white	415	silver grey	3347	med yellow green		
744	pale yellow	312	v. dk baby blue	317	silver grey		
3325	lt baby blue	318	lt silver grey	3346	dk yellow green		

ROBIN KEY

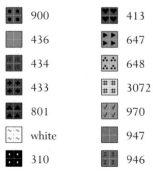

900		413	
436		647	
434		648	
433		3072	
801		970	
white		947	
310		946	

BLUE TIT KEY

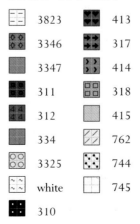

3823		413	
3346		317	
3347		414	
311		318	
312		415	
334		762	
3325		744	
white		745	
310			

FOREST CREATURES

A WONDERFUL MIXTURE OF ANIMALS, large and small, make up the collection of designs in this picture. The central portrait is of a magnificent brown bear, the water foaming around him as he fishes for salmon. Surrounding him are two delightful young bear cubs and the lovely doe-eyed head of a roe deer. There is also a bright-eyed stoat, a fierce little mammal. His black-tipped tail is one of the features that tells him apart from the weasel – see his portrait on page 53. A brightly coloured greater spotted woodpecker also features in the design and yet another little bandit, the racoon, who is as much at home now in a town as he is the forest.

The other three designs that make up this forest collection are a beautiful young puma padding softly forwards, and two lovely foxes just emerging from a hedge of grasses. To finish, there is a regal looking red stag with a valley scene behind him.

Forest Creatures

Prepare your fabric for work and mark the centre point (see Workbox). Follow the chart on pages 54–57, using two strands of stranded cotton (floss) for all cross stitch, worked over two threads of evenweave fabric.

Work the backstitches in one strand of black 310 stranded cotton (floss) for the brown bear's eye, stoat's eye, roe deer's eye and greater spotted woodpecker's eye. Work the French knots in one strand of white for the eye highlights on the stoat, roe deer, greater spotted woodpecker and racoon.

Mount and frame your picture to complete or see Display It, page 70.

STITCH IT

Fabric:	*28 count sage green Zweigart Brittney 59 x 59cm (23 x 23in)*
Threads:	*DMC stranded cotton (floss)*
Stitch count:	*209 x 209*
Design size:	*38 x 38cm (15 x 15in) approx*
Stitches:	*Whole cross stitch, three-quarter cross stitch, backstitch, French knots*

FOREST CREATURES THREAD LIST

1 skein each DMC stranded cotton (floss)

310	black	976	med rust	318	lt silver grey	3782	lt mocha brown
502	blue green	437	lt tan	951	lt tawny	3823	ultra pale yellow
3371	black brown	977	lt rust	415	silver grey	3032	med mocha brown
501	dk blue green	738	v. lt tan	934	black avocado green	732	olive green
938	ultra dk coffee brown	3827	v. lt rust	762	v. lt silver grey	3781	dk mocha brown
500	v. dk blue green	739	ultra v. lt tan	937	med avocado green	733	med olive green
898	v. dk coffee brown	838	v. dk beige brown	869	v. dk hazelnut brown	610	dk drab brown
3790	ultra dk beige grey	746	off white	470	lt avocado green	734	lt olive green
801	dk coffee brown	839	dk beige brown	420	dk hazelnut brown	611	drab brown
632	ultra v. dk desert sand	3799	v. dk pewter grey	817	v. dk coral red	775	v. lt baby blue
433	med brown golden	840	med beige brown	3828	hazelnut brown	612	lt drab brown
300	v. dk mahogany	413	dk silver grey	349	dk peach	504	lt blue green
434	lt brown golden	841	lt beige brown	422	lt hazelnut brown	613	v. lt drab brown
975	v. dk rust	317	silver grey	815	med garnet	3813	lt blue green
435	v. lt brown golden	842	v. lt beige brown	676	lt golden sand	3033	v. lt mocha brown
3826	dk rust	414	dk silver grey	822	lt beige grey	503	med blue green
436	tan	543	ultra v. lt beige brown	677	v. lt golden sand	644	med beige grey

2 skeins each DMC stranded cotton (floss)

blanc	white

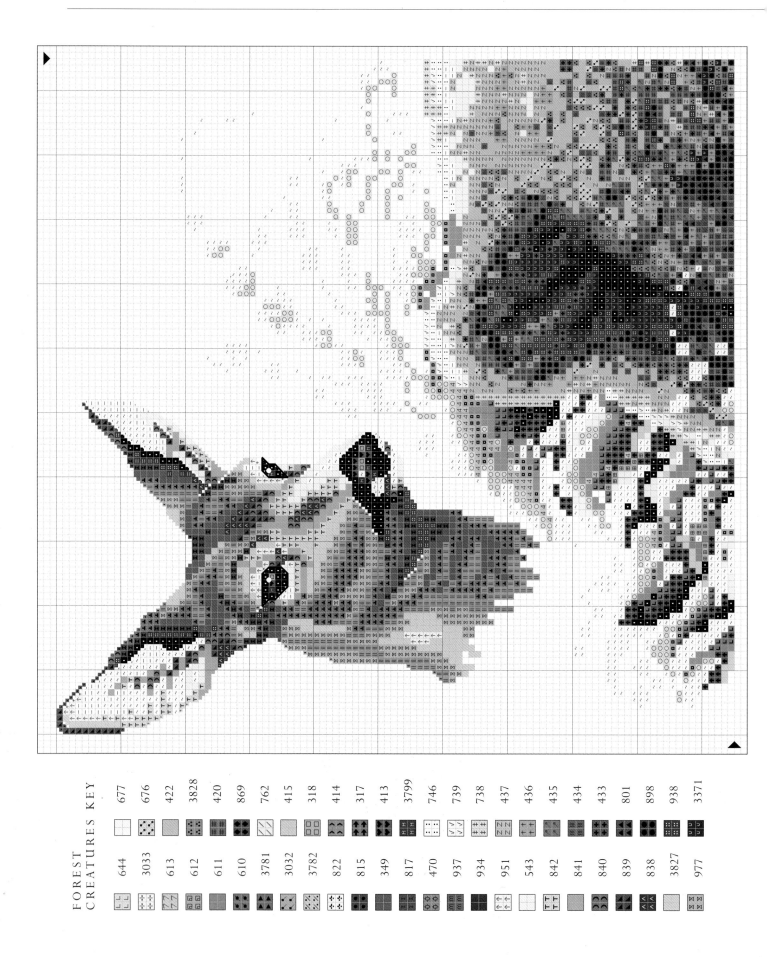

| 677 | 676 | 422 | 3828 | 420 | 869 | 762 | 415 | 318 | 414 | 317 | 413 | 3799 | 746 | 739 | 738 | 437 | 436 | 435 | 434 | 433 | 801 | 898 | 938 | 3371 |

| 644 | 3033 | 613 | 612 | 611 | 610 | 3781 | 3032 | 3782 | 822 | 815 | 349 | 817 | 470 | 937 | 934 | 951 | 543 | 842 | 841 | 840 | 839 | 838 | 3827 | 977 |

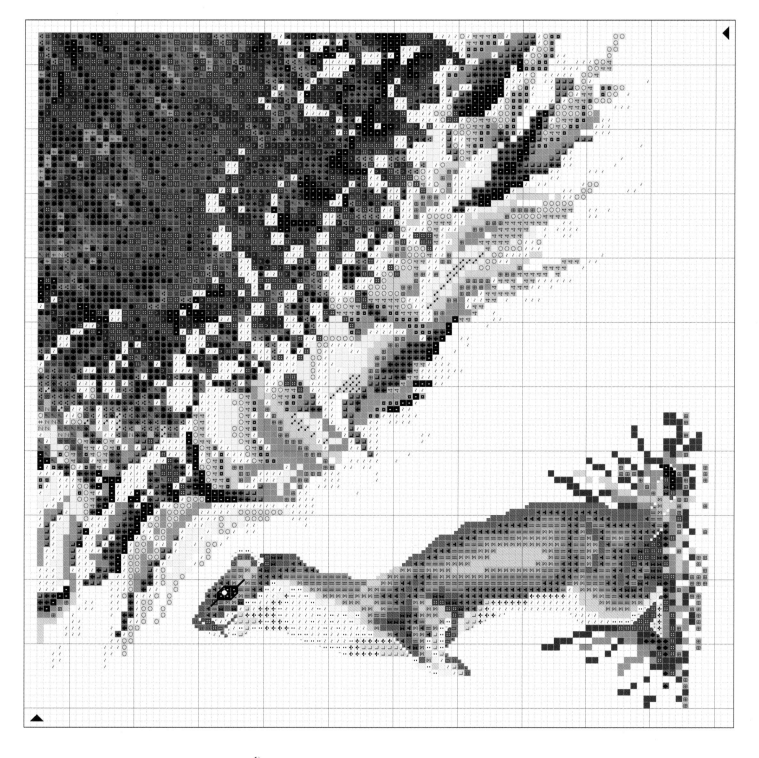

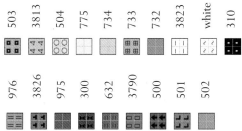

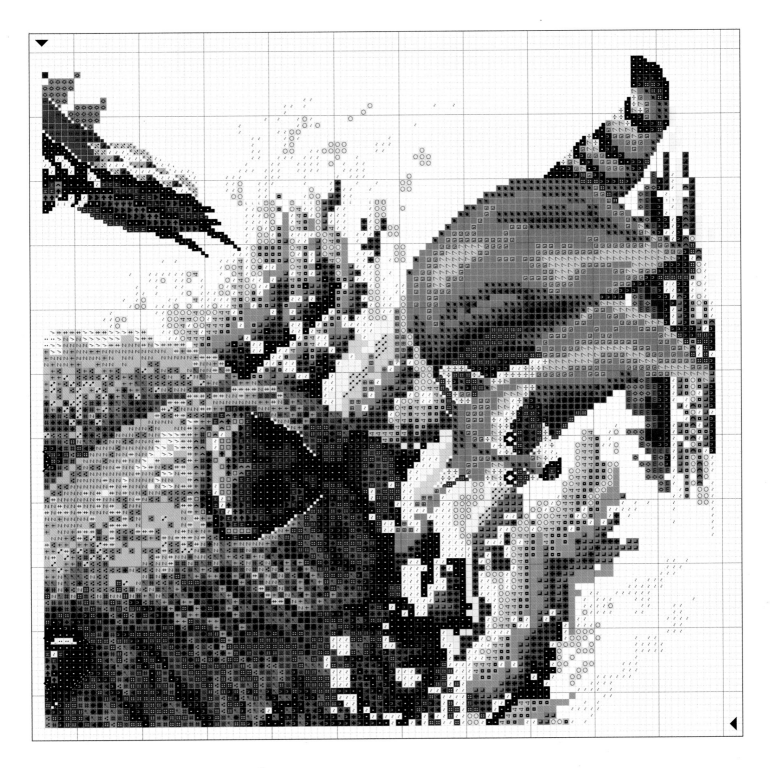

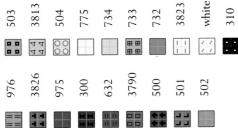

Puma

ONE OF THE MOST LOVELY of the big cats, the puma, ranges far and wide over the world and is also known as mountain lion or cougar. As a general rule, pumas are bigger in the colder parts of their range and smaller in the tropics, but are equally at home in the desert or above the snow line. Pumas have always been notable for their generally neutral attitude to man. If captured when young, they are easily tamed. Like domestic cats, they can amuse themselves for hours with balls of wool and toys, and they will purr when petted.

STITCH IT

Fabric:	*14 count white Aida 41 x 48cm (16 x 19in)*
Threads:	*DMC stranded cotton (floss) (see thread list page 69)*
Stitch count:	*105 x 150*
Design size:	*21 x 28cm (8 x 11in) approx*
Stitches:	*Whole cross stitch, long stitch*

Prepare your fabric for work and mark the centre point (see Workbox). Follow the chart on pages 60/61, using two strands of stranded cotton (floss) for all cross stitch. Work the long stitches for the whiskers using one strand of white (shown in black on the chart for clarity).

Mount and frame your picture to complete or see Display It, page 70.

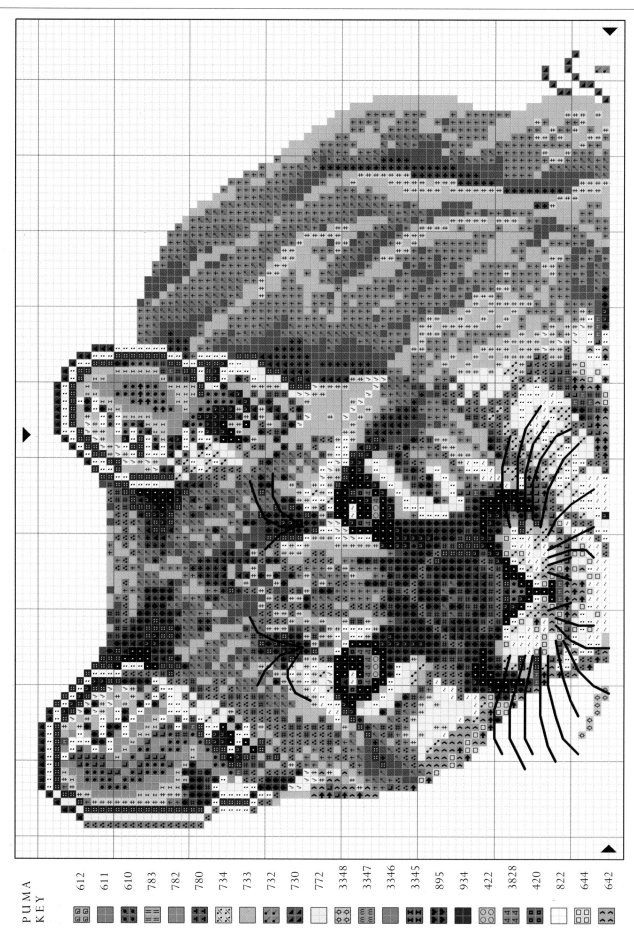

PUMA
KEY

| 612 | 611 | 610 | 783 | 782 | 780 | 734 | 733 | 732 | 730 | 772 | 3348 | 3347 | 3346 | 3345 | 895 | 934 | 422 | 3828 | 420 | 822 | 644 | 642 |

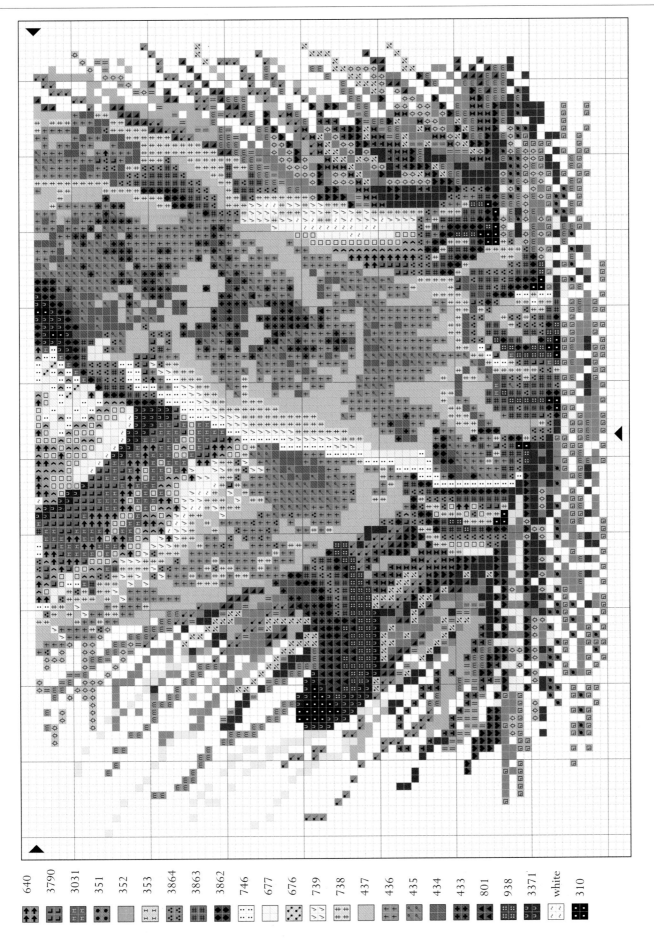

640 3790 3031 351 352 353 3864 3863 3862 746 677 676 739 738 437 436 435 434 433 801 938 3371 white 310

Foxes

FOXES NEVER CEASE TO AMAZE ME: they now are as common living in town as in the countryside. They appear all over the world from the arctic to the desert, surviving in the harshest of environments. I have spent many happy hours watching these adorable animals. In this design I have an adult in the foreground emerging from a grassy bank with one of her fully grown cubs looking as if he wants to race ahead.

STITCH IT

Fabric:	*14 count khaki Aida 41 x 54cm (16 x 21in)*
Threads:	*DMC stranded cotton (floss) (see thread list page 69)*
Stitch count:	*110 x 180*
Design size:	*21 x 33cm (8 x 13in) approx*
Stitches:	*Whole cross stitch, three-quarter cross stitch, backstitch*

Prepare your fabric for work and mark the centre point (see Workbox). Follow the chart on pages 64/65, using two strands of stranded cotton (floss) for all cross stitch. Work the grass stem backstitches in one strand of 898.

Mount and frame your picture to complete or see Display It, page 70.

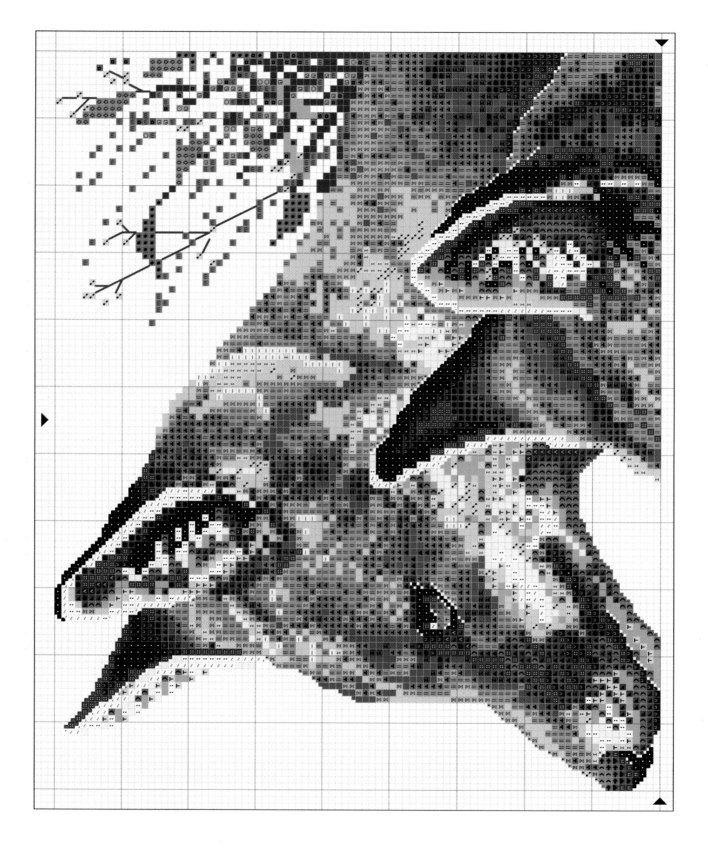

FOXES
KEY   783 782 780 833 832 831 829 471 470 469 937 934 436 435 434

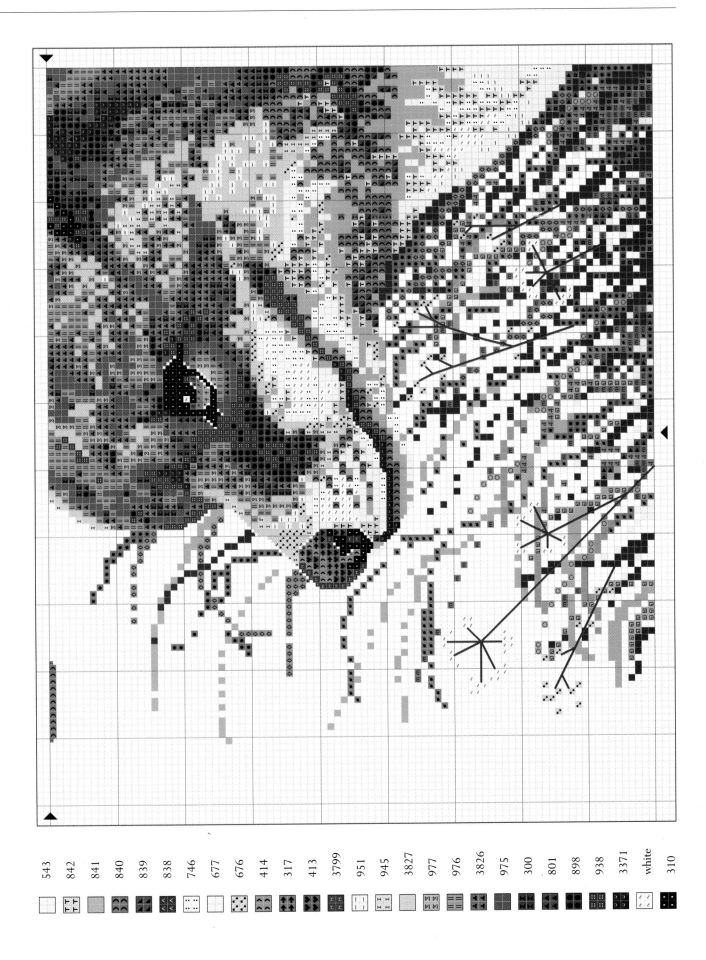

543 842 841 840 839 838 746 677 676 414 317 413 3799 951 945 3827 977 976 3826 975 300 801 898 938 3371 white 310

Red Stag

THIS DESIGN SHOWS a handsome red stag standing proudly in his valley. For most of the year the stags live apart from the hinds (females), occupying a well-defined territory. They shed their antlers in the spring. New antlers soon sprout and are fully grown, bearing up to twelve points, by autumn. Shortly after this the stag will round up the hinds to mate with them, guarding them carefully when any other stag comes too close.

Prepare your fabric for work and mark the centre point (see Workbox). Follow the chart on page 68, using two strands of stranded cotton (floss) for all cross stitch. Work the French knots in one strand of white for the eye highlights.

Mount and frame your picture to complete or see Display It, page 70.

STITCH IT

Fabric:	*14 count sky blue Aida 38 x 42cm (15 x 16½in)*
Threads:	*DMC stranded cotton (floss) (see thread list on page 69)*
Stitch count:	*100 x 115*
Design size:	*19 x 22cm (7 x 8½in) approx*
Stitches:	*Whole cross stitch, three-quarter cross stitch, French knots*

▲	801	#	3864	H	3799		772	∧	935	∴	833	⊠	471
⬥	938	◆	3863	–	746	#	3051	▪	3345		834	‖	472
∪	3371		3862	–	677		3052		3346		3790		
~	white	√	739	∴	422	L	3053	4	3347		932		
▪	310	‡	738		3828	#	317	○	3348	∴	3753		

RED STAG KEY

PUMA THREAD LIST
1 skein each DMC stranded cotton (floss)

310	black	434	lt brown golden	676	lt golden sand	353	v. lt peach
642	dk beige grey	934	black avocado green	772	v. lt yellow green	782	dk topaz
blanc	white	435	v. lt brown golden	677	v. lt golden sand	352	lt peach
644	med beige grey	895	v. dk hunter green	730	v. dk olive green	783	med topaz
3371	black brown	436	tan	746	off white	351	peach
822	lt beige grey	3345	v. dk yellow green	732	olive green	610	dk drab brown
938	ultra dk coffee brown	437	lt tan	3862	dk brown	3031	v. dk mocha brown
420	dk hazelnut brown	3346	dk yellow green	733	med olive green	611	drab brown
801	dk coffee brown	738	v. lt tan	3863	med brown	3790	ultra dk beige brown
3828	hazelnut brown	3347	med yellow green	734	lt olive green	612	lt drab brown
433	med brown golden	739	ultra v. lt tan	3864	lt brown	640	v. dk beige grey
422	lt hazelnut brown	3348	lt yellow green	780	ultra v. dk topaz		

FOXES THREAD LIST
1 skein each DMC stranded cotton (floss)

310	black	543	ultra v. lt beige brown	3827	v. lt rust	832	golden olive
838	v. dk beige brown	300	v. dk mahogany	469	avocado green	414	dk silver grey
blanc	white	434	lt brown golden	945	tawny	833	lt golden olive
839	dk beige brown	975	v. dk rust	470	lt avocado green	676	lt golden sand
3371	black brown	435	v. lt brown golden	951	lt tawny	780	ultra v. dk topaz
840	med beige brown	3826	dk rust	471	v. lt avocado green	677	v. lt golden sand
938	ultra dk coffee brown	436	tan	3799	v. dk pewter grey	782	dk topaz
841	lt beige brown	976	med rust	829	v. dk golden olive	746	off white
898	v. dk coffee brown	934	black avocado green	413	dk silver grey	783	med topaz
842	v. lt beige brown	977	lt rust	831	med golden olive		
801	dk coffee brown	937	med avocado green	317	silver grey		

RED STAG THREAD LIST
1 skein each DMC stranded cotton (floss)

310	black	801	dk coffee brown	3863	med brown	677	v. lt golden sand
3053	green grey	3348	lt yellow green	935	dk avocado green	834	v. lt golden olive
blanc	white	738	v. lt tan	3864	lt brown	746	off white
3052	med green grey	3347	med yellow green	3753	ultra v. lt antique blue	833	lt golden olive
3371	black brown	739	ultra v. lt tan	3828	hazelnut brown	3799	v. dk pewter grey
3051	dk green grey	3346	dk yellow green	932	lt antique blue	472	ultra lt avocado green
938	ultra dk coffee brown	3862	dk brown	422	lt hazelnut brown	317	silver grey
772	v. lt yellow green	3345	v. dk yellow green	3790	ultra dk beige grey	471	v. lt avocado green

DISPLAY IT

There are some lovely designs in this section, perfect for use on all sorts of items. The main Forest Creatures design could be made up into an impressive square cushion, while the handsome foxes would make a wonderful rectangular cushion (see page 124 for instructions). To give an added dimension in the foxes design, the cross stitches of the grass seed-heads could be replaced with similarly coloured French knots or beads. The roe deer head and the stoat would make lovely small pictures. The puma would look wonderful stitched up into a doorstop on a 10 count Aida fabric (see page 125 for instructions) or could be stitched on canvas in a larger count for a superb rug or wall hanging (see pages 119 and 126 for instructions). If you stitch the design on canvas, remember to choose a complementary colour wool (yarn) to fill the background.

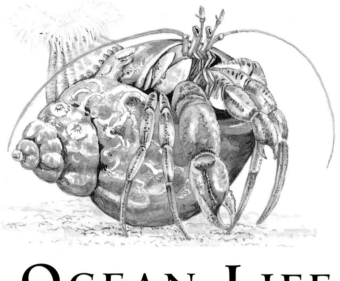

OCEAN LIFE

A WONDERFUL DOLPHIN is the central motif for this opening design for life in the ocean. I had such a wide variety to choose from, that I decided in the end on a mixture of large and small. The largest is the whale shark, a beautiful, plankton eater that little is known about. The smallest is the hermit crab: as he grows he finds a vacant shell and moves in as fast as he can, as this is when he is most vulnerable. A group of dolphins leaping joyfully, and a small shoal of tropical blue-lined snappers add movement to the design. Three delicate jellyfish round off the collection. To make the jellyfish look more delicate, they are stitched with only one strand of stranded cotton (floss).

The three other designs that make up the ocean life collection are quite unusual and versatile – see Display It on page 92 for just a few ideas. There is a mass of baby turtles emerging from the sand, then an abstract design of a shoal of mackerel, and to finish a magnificent humpback whale and calf.

Ocean Life

STITCH IT

Fabric: *28 count blue Zweigart Brittney*
                   59 x 59cm (23 x 23in)

Threads: *DMC stranded cotton (floss)*

Stitch count: *209 x 209*

Design size: *38 x 38cm (15 x 15in) approx*

Stitches: *Whole cross stitch, three-quarter*
                   cross stitch, backstitch, French knots

Prepare your fabric for work and mark the centre point (see Workbox). Follow the chart on pages 76–79, working over two threads of evenweave fabric, using two strands of stranded cotton (floss) for all the cross stitch except the jellyfish which is worked with one strand.

Work all the backstitches with one strand. Use black 310 for the main dolphin's mouth and the hermit crab's eyes. Use 3799 around the bodies of the dolphin group. Use 535 for the eyes and mouths of the shoal of fish and 3750 for the body stripes. Use 3046 and 3045 for the jellyfish tendrils. Work the French knots with two strands of white for the eye highlights on the fish shoal and the hermit crab.

Mount and frame your picture to complete or see Display It, page 92.

OCEAN LIFE THREAD LIST
1 skein each DMC stranded cotton (floss)

310	black	762	v. lt pearl grey	775	v. lt baby blue	519	sky blue
725	topaz	370	med mustard	975	v. dk rust	3045	dk yellow beige
3799	v. dk pewter grey	3750	v. dk antique blue	3809	v. dk turquoise	3761	lt sky blue
800	pale delft blue	371	mustard	801	dk coffee brown	3756	ultra v. lt baby blue
413	dk silver grey	930	dk antique blue	3810	dk turquoise	ecru	ecru
809	delft blue	372	lt mustard	938	ultra dk coffee brown	928	v. lt grey green
317	silver grey	931	med antique blue	939	v. dk navy blue	3078	v. lt golden yellow
453	lt shell grey	3827	v. lt rust	738	v. lt tan	927	lt grey green
414	dk silver grey	932	lt antique blue	517	dk wedgewood	727	v. lt topaz
452	med shell grey	977	lt rust	437	lt tan	729	med golden sand
318	lt silver grey	3752	v. lt antique blue	3760	med wedgewood	726	lt topaz
451	dk shell grey	976	med rust	3047	lt yellow beige		
415	silver grey	3753	ultra v. lt antique blue	518	lt wedgewood		
535	v. lt ash grey	3826	dk rust	3046	med yellow beige		

2 skeins each DMC stranded cotton (floss)

blanc	white

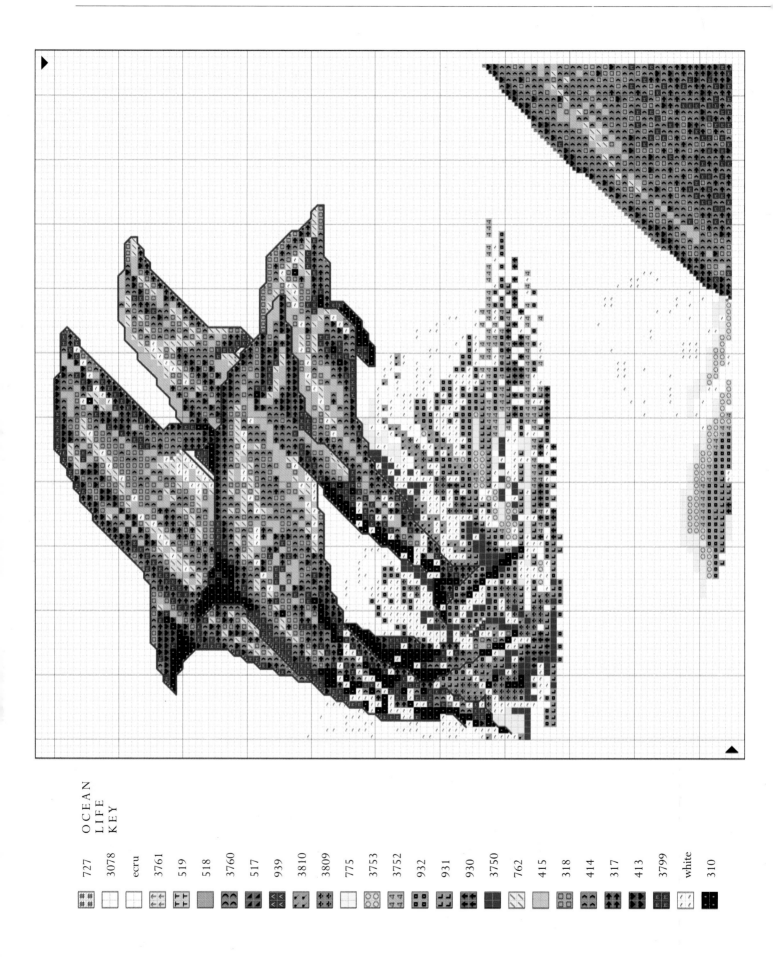

OCEAN
LIFE
KEY

727 3078 ecru 3761 519 518 3760 517 939 3810 3809 775 3753 3752 932 931 930 3750 762 415 318 414 317 413 3799 white 310

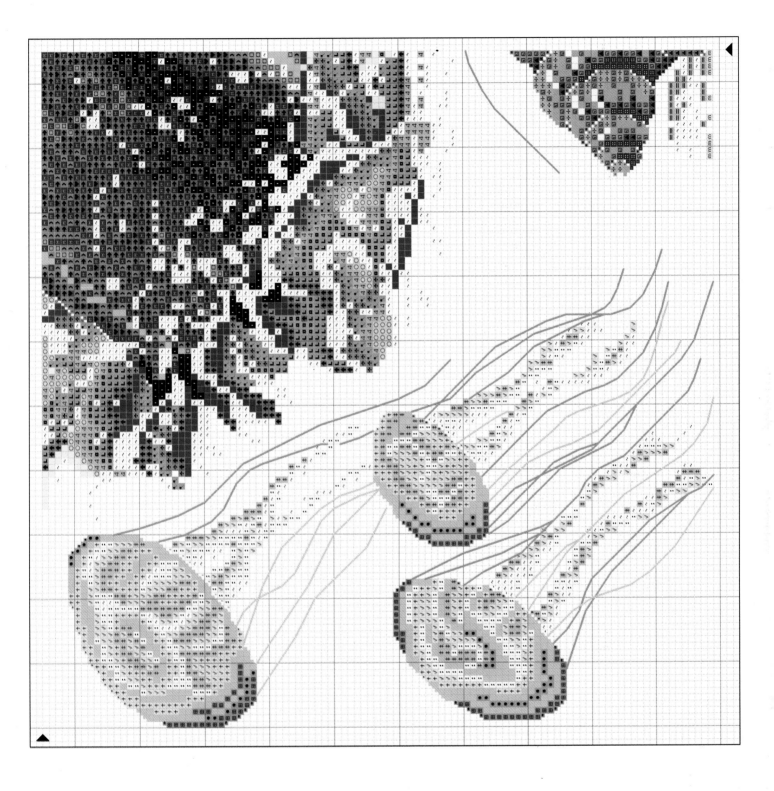

729 927 928 3756 3045 3046 3047 437 738 938 801 975 3826 976 977 3827 372 371 370 535 451 452 453 809 800 725 726

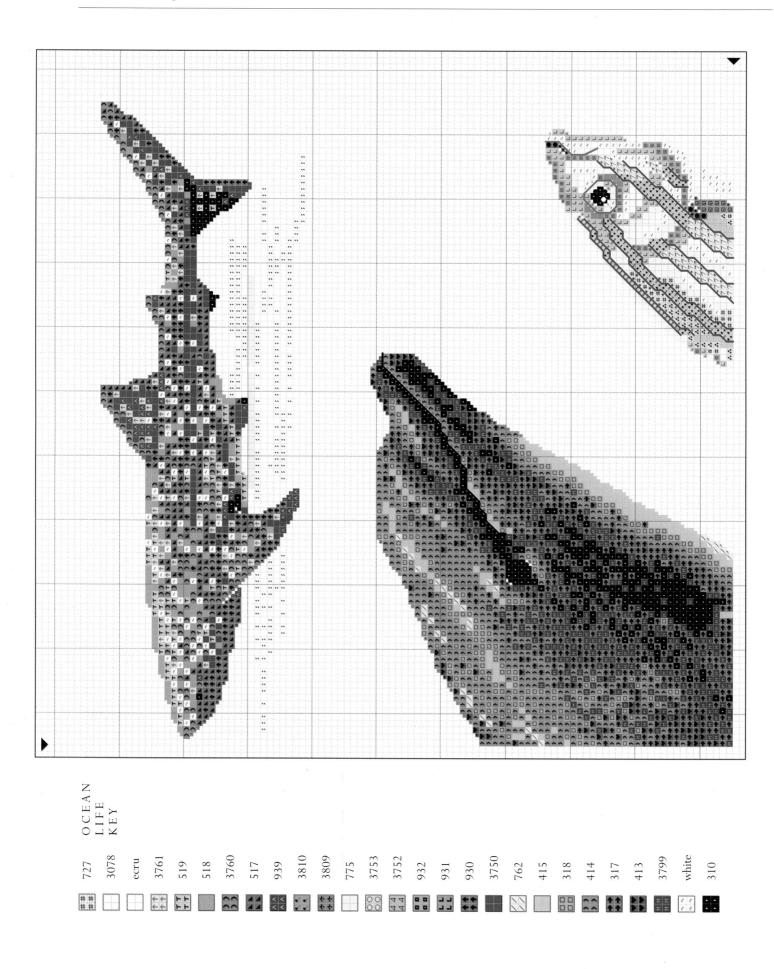

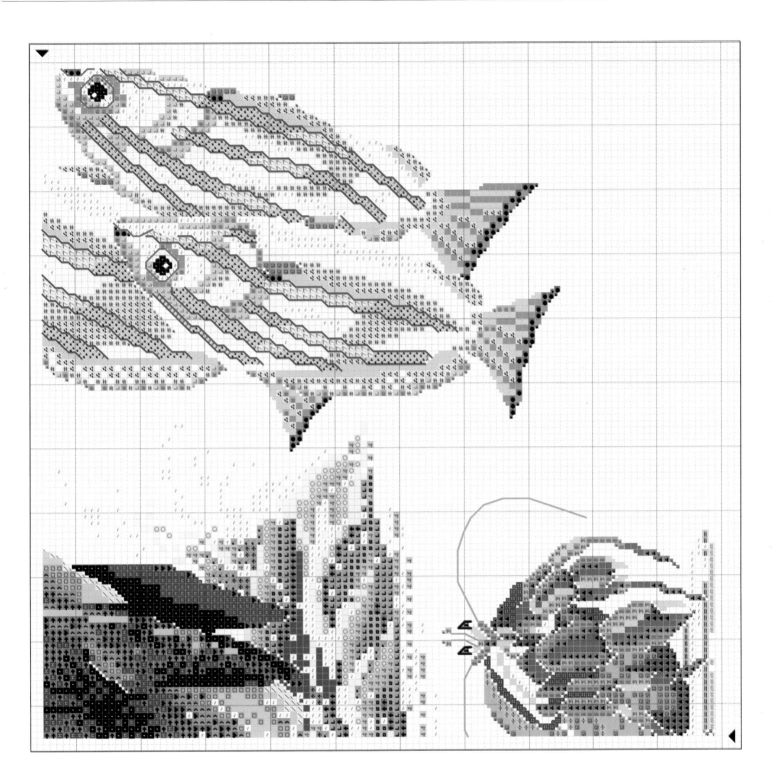

729 927 928 3756 3045 3046 3047 437 738 938 801 975 3826 976 977 3827 372 371 370 535 451 452 453 809 800 725 726

Baby Turtles

THIS UTTERLY DELIGHTFUL heap of baby turtles
emerging from the sand after hatching are
beginning their mad rush to the sea and
hopefully to survival. So many are born but with
so many hazards to overcome, very few survive.
This design is very versatile, as it can be stitched
as a whole or you can take a portion of it and
use it to decorate a towel border. The blue
arrows on the chart indicate the border width
when using the design for an Aida band (see
page 119 for using embroidery bands).

STITCH IT

Fabric:	*14 count white Aida*
	48 x 41cm (18¾ x16¼in)
Threads:	*DMC stranded cotton (floss)*
	(see thread list page 91)
Stitch count:	*150 x 110*
Design size:	*27 x 20cm (10¾ x 8in) approx*
Stitches:	*Whole cross stitch, three-quarter cross stitch, backstitch*

Prepare your fabric for work and mark the centre
point (see Workbox). Follow the chart on pages
82/83, using two strands of stranded cotton (floss)
for all cross stitch. Work the 3799 backstitch in
one strand of stranded cotton (floss).

Mount and frame your picture to complete or
see Display It, page 92.

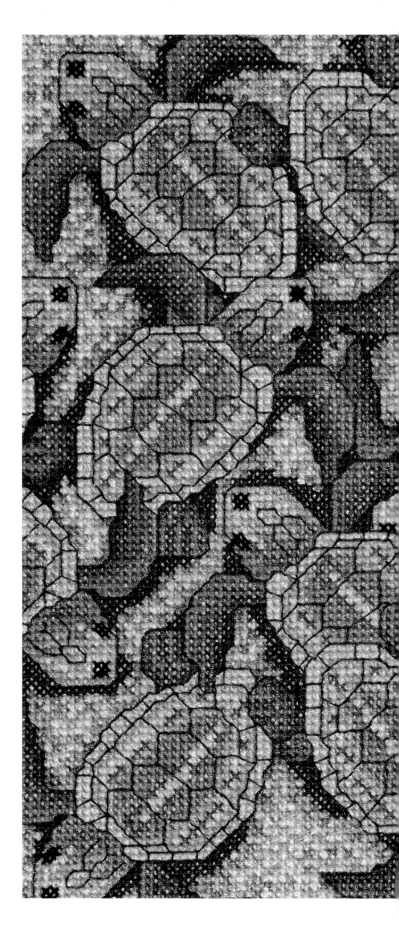

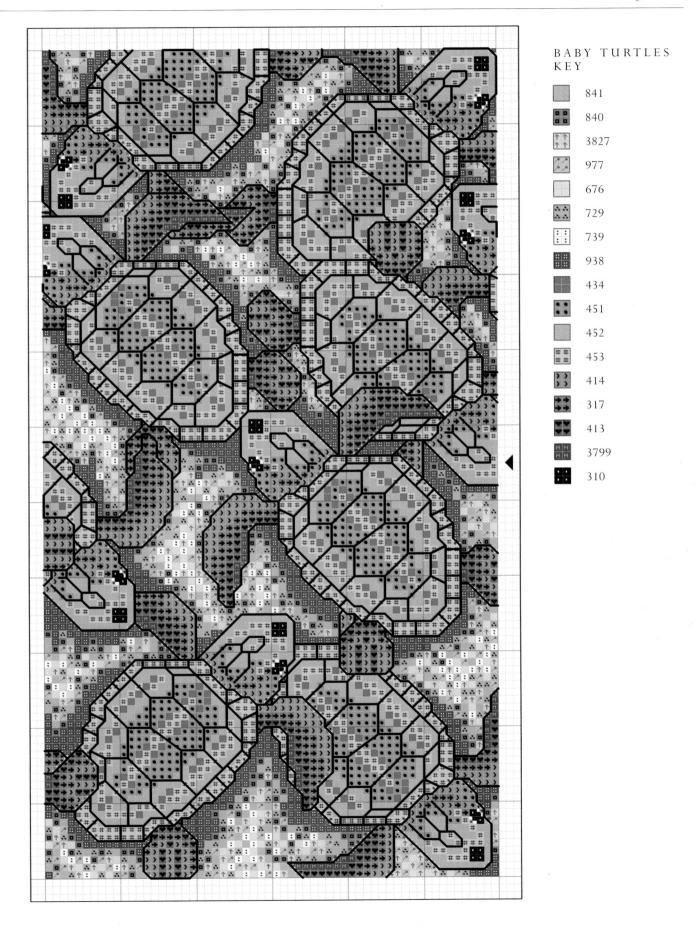

BABY TURTLES
KEY

	841
	840
	3827
	977
	676
	729
	739
	938
	434
	451
	452
	453
	414
	317
	413
	3799
	310

Mackerel Shoal

MACKEREL WERE MY INSPIRATION for this design with their gorgeous colouring. A mass of fish makes this composition quite abstract. As with the turtles, this design is versatile and can be used whole or in part, for example as a towel border. The blue arrows on the chart refer to the border width when using the design for an Aida band (see page 119 for using embroidery bands).

STITCH IT

Fabric:	*14 count white Aida 48 x 41cm (18¾ x 16in)*
Threads:	*DMC stranded cotton (floss) (see thread list page 91)*
Stitch count:	*150 x 110*
Design size:	*27 x 20cm (10¾ x 8in) approx*
Stitches:	*Whole cross stitch*

Prepare your fabric for work and mark the centre point (see Workbox). Follow the chart on pages 86/87, using two strands of stranded cotton (floss) for all cross stitch.

Mount and frame your picture to complete or see Display It, page 92.

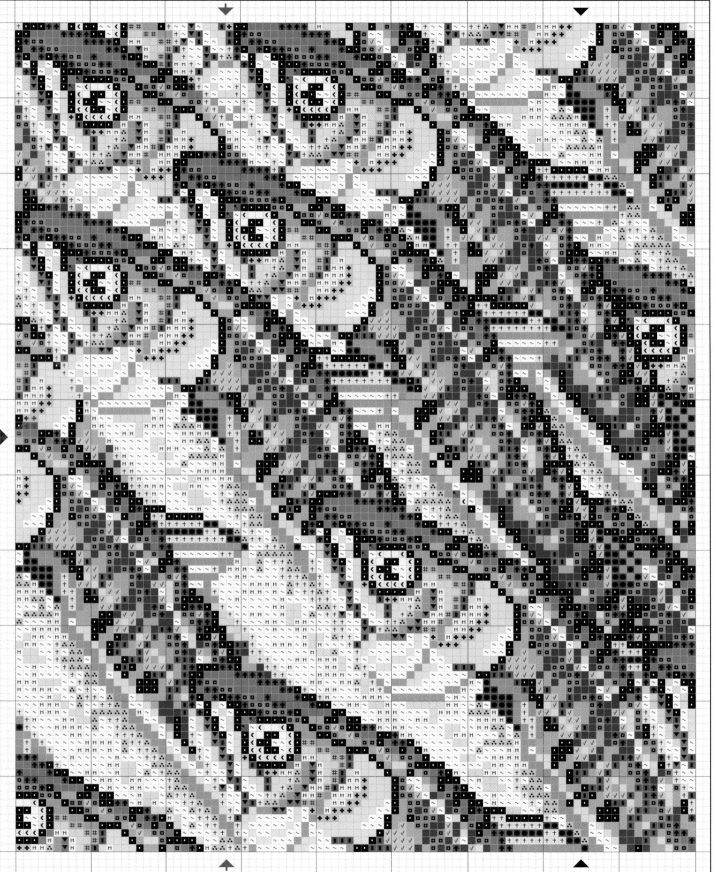

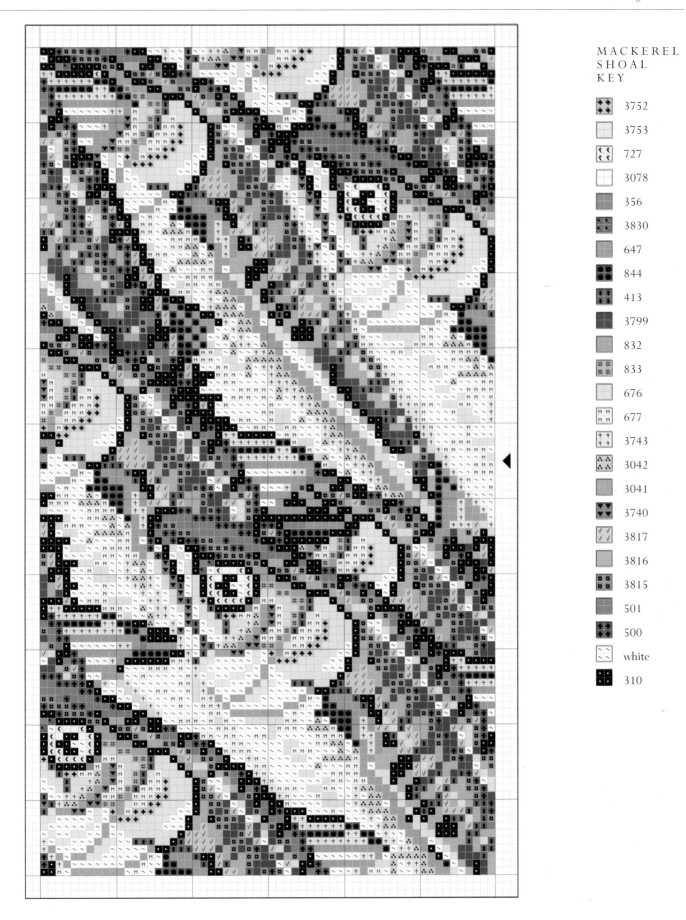

MACKEREL
SHOAL
KEY

✛✛	3752
	3753
‹‹	727
	3078
	356
	3830
	647
●	844
❙❙	413
	3799
	832
# #	833
	676
н н	677
✛✛	3743
∴∴	3042
	3041
▼▼	3740
√√	3817
	3816
▫▫	3815
	501
↑↑	500
~ ~	white
●	310

Humpback Whale and Calf

THIS MAGNIFICENT HUMPBACK WHALE and calf are shown here stitched on cadet blue Aida to imply the ocean depths, with air bubbles trailing behind them as they dive down from the surface. An adult whale can weigh up to forty tons. The creature is also remarkable for its extremely long flippers, which can be up to a third of its body length. Humpback whales assemble each year around the Hawaiian Islands to breed. After giving birth, mating and their wonderful bouts of singing, the whales then return to the seas off Alaska to feed on krill.

STITCH IT

Fabric:	*14 count cadet blue Aida* *38 x 37cm (15 x 14½in)*
Threads:	*DMC stranded cotton (floss)* *(see thread list page 91)*
Stitch count:	*100 x 92*
Design size:	*18 x 17cm (7 x 6½in) approx*
Stitches:	*Whole cross stitch,* *three-quarter cross stitch*

Prepare your fabric for work and mark the centre point (see Workbox). Follow the chart on page 90, using two strands of stranded cotton (floss) for all cross stitch. If preferred, you can use beads or French knots to replace all the white cross stitches. If you do use beads, choose a colour that matches or is complementary to the thread colour you are replacing (see Adding Beads page 118).

Mount and frame your picture to complete or see Display It, page 92.

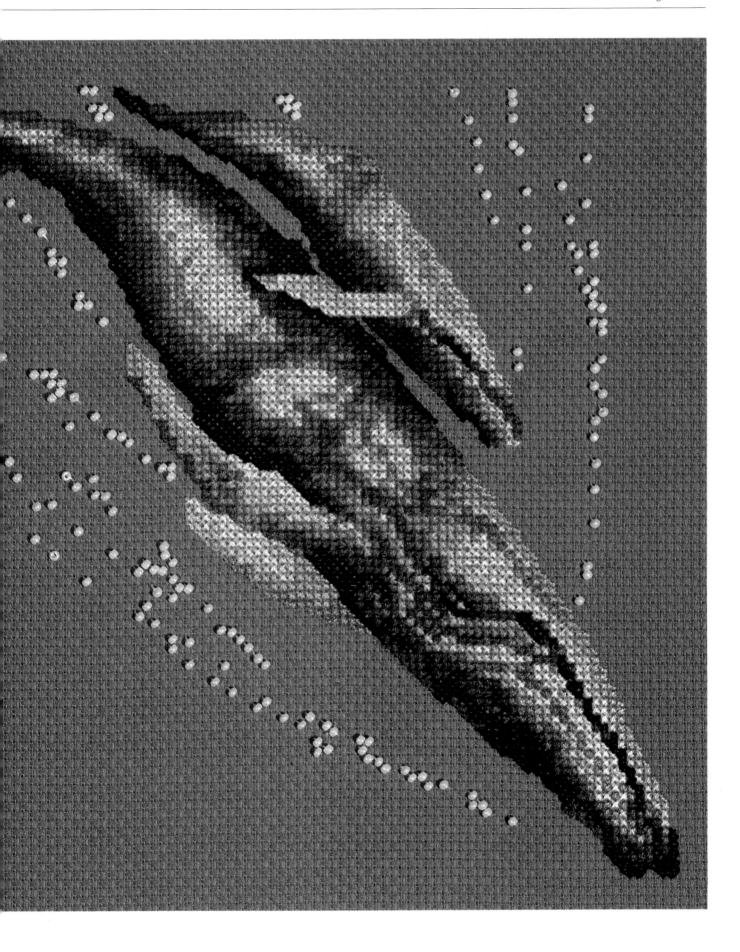

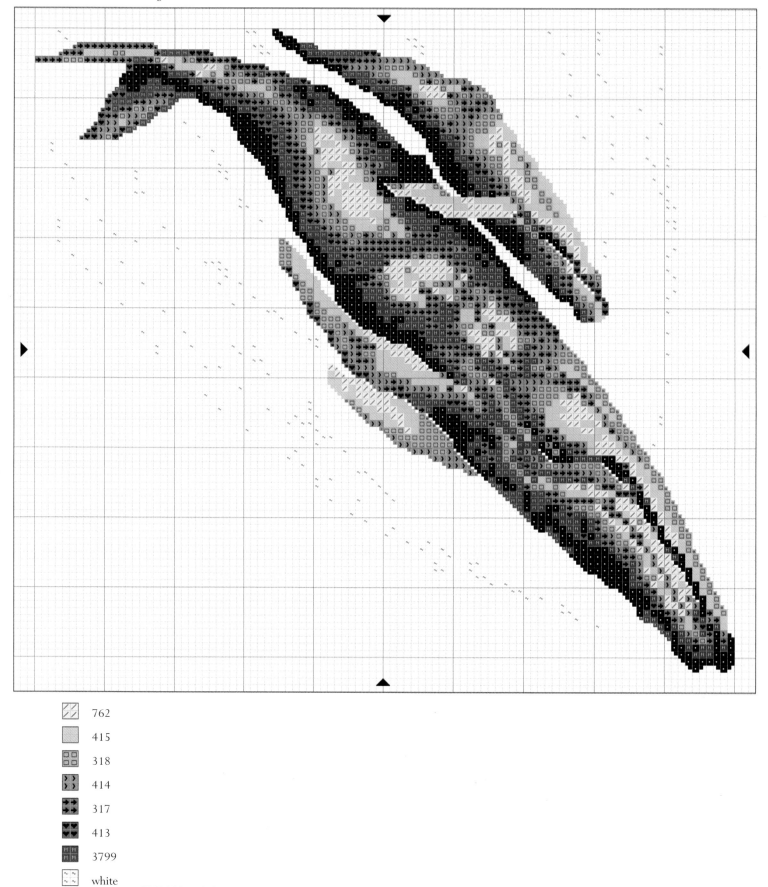

	762
	415
	318
	414
	317
	413
	3799
	white
	310

HUMPBACK WHALE
AND CALF KEY

BABY TURTLES THREAD LIST
1 skein each DMC stranded cotton (floss)

310	black	413	dk silver grey	414	dk silver grey	434	lt golden brown
739	ultra v. lt tan	676	lt golden sand	3827	v. lt rust	841	lt beige brown
3799	v. dk pewter grey	317	silver grey	451	dk shell grey	938	ultra dk coffee brown
729	med golden sand	977	lt rust	840	med beige brown		

2 skeins each DMC stranded cotton (floss)

453	lt shell grey
452	med shell grey

MACKEREL SHOAL THREAD LIST
1 skein each DMC stranded cotton (floss)

500	v. dk blue green	3816	med celadon green	3041	med silver plum	677	v. lt golden sand
832	golden olive	844	ultra dk beaver brown	356	med terra cotta	3753	ultra v. lt antique blue
501	dk blue green	3817	lt celadon green	3042	lt silver plum	676	lt golden sand
3799	v. dk pewter grey	647	med beaver grey	3078	v. lt golden yellow	3752	v. lt antique blue
3815	dk celadon green	3740	dk silver plum	3743	v. lt silver plum	833	lt golden olive
413	dk silver grey	3830	terra cotta	727	v. lt topaz		

2 skeins each DMC stranded cotton (floss)

310	black
blanc	white

HUMPBACK WHALE AND CALF THREAD LIST
1 skein each DMC stranded cotton (floss)

310	black	318	lt silver grey	413	dk silver grey
414	dk silver grey	3799	v. dk pewter grey	762	v. lt pearl grey
blanc	white	415	silver grey	317	silver grey

DISPLAY IT

Each of the individual motifs that make up the
Ocean Life opening design could be stitched
separately to make a lovely set of pictures for a
bathroom. The hermit crab could be stitched on a
small square of Aida, edged with a complementary
coloured bias binding and stitched onto a towel.
Stitched up in a larger count it would also make a
super bath mat. The turtle and mackerel designs
could be inset into a box (shown on page 2),
stitched on a complementary coloured Aida, such
as a parchment colour. It is also possible to stitch a
single turtle, which can then be used for mugs and
cards. Pick the most complete turtle in the design;
this may have a foot missing but just take the
missing part of the design from another turtle. The
turtles are all the same, just over- and under-laid,
turned and reversed to make up the design.

POLAR WILDLIFE

A LOVELY GREY SEAL with soft, appealing eyes just about to pull herself from the foaming waves onto the shore is the central design for my polar collection. The female grey seal may live for about thirty-five years and the male for about twenty-five. Surrounding her is a mother polar bear with cub and a wonderful orca leaping out of the sea into the air. An arctic fox in his winter white coat, a mother and baby common seal and two emperor penguins also feature in the design. Each of the motifs can be stitched on their own or framed as small pictures, like the orca on page 97. There are more ideas on how to use the designs in Display It, on page 114.

There are also three additional designs in this collection: a fabulous head and shoulder study of a wolf; a charming group of Adélie penguins diving off an icy ledge into the sea; and lastly a superb mountain hare on a snow-laden mountain landscape, his snowy coat perfectly complemented by icy blue Aida.

Polar Wildlife

STITCH IT

Fabric:	*28 count dove grey Zweigart Brittney 59 x 59cm (23 x 23in)*
Threads:	*DMC stranded cotton (floss)*
Stitch count:	*209 x 209*
Design size:	*38 x 38cm (15 x 15in) approx*
Stitches:	*Whole cross stitch, three-quarter cross stitch, backstitch, French knots, long stitch*

Prepare your fabric for work and mark the centre point (see Workbox). Follow the chart on pages 98–101, using two strands of stranded cotton (floss) for cross stitch, worked over two threads of evenweave fabric.

Work the backstitch in one strand of 310 for the main seal's eyes, the mother seal and cub mouths and the arctic fox's eye. Work the French knots in one strand of white for the eye highlights on the emperor penguins and the arctic fox. Work the long stitches in one strand of white for the main seal's whiskers and eyebrows (shown in black on the chart).

Mount and frame your picture to complete or see Display It, page 114.

POLAR COLLECTION THREAD LIST

1 skein each DMC stranded cotton (floss)

3799	v. dk pewter grey	762	v. lt pearl grey	841	lt beige brown	3032	med mocha brown
712	cream	503	med blue green	676	lt golden sand	742	lt tangerine
413	dk silver grey	ecru	ecru	842	v. lt beige brown	3782	lt mocha brown
3866	beige	3813	lt blue green	677	v. lt golden sand	743	med yellow
317	silver grey	3371	black brown	543	ultra v. lt beige brown	3033	v. lt mocha brown
822	lt beige grey	504	lt blue green	746	off white	744	pale yellow
414	dk silver grey	838	v. dk beige brown	3862	dk brown	945	tawny
500	v. dk blue green	420	dk hazelnut brown	918	dk red copper	745	lt pale yellow
318	lt silver grey	839	dk beige brown	3863	med brown	738	v. lt tawny
501	dk blue green	3828	hazelnut brown	740	tangerine	3823	v. pale yellow
415	silver grey	840	med beige brown	3864	lt brown	739	ultra v. lt tan
502	blue green	729	med golden sand	741	med tangerine		

2 skeins each DMC stranded cotton (floss)

310	black

3 skeins each DMC stranded cotton (floss)

blanc	white

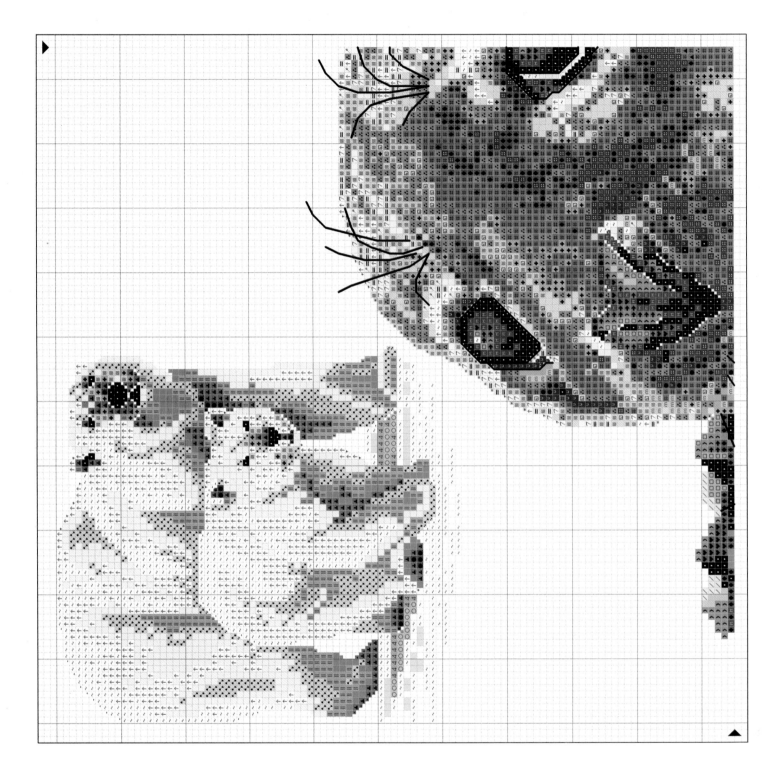

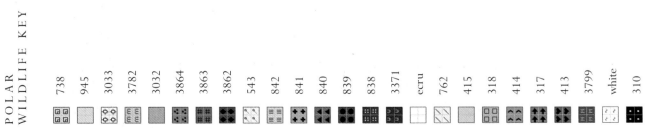

3823　745　744　743　742　741　740　918　746　677　676　729　3828　420　504　3813　503　502　501　500　822　3866　712　739

POLAR
WILDLIFE KEY

| 738 | 945 | 3033 | 3782 | 3032 | 3864 | 3863 | 3862 | 543 | 842 | 841 | 840 | 839 | 838 | 3371 | ecru | 762 | 415 | 318 | 414 | 317 | 413 | 3799 | white | 310 |

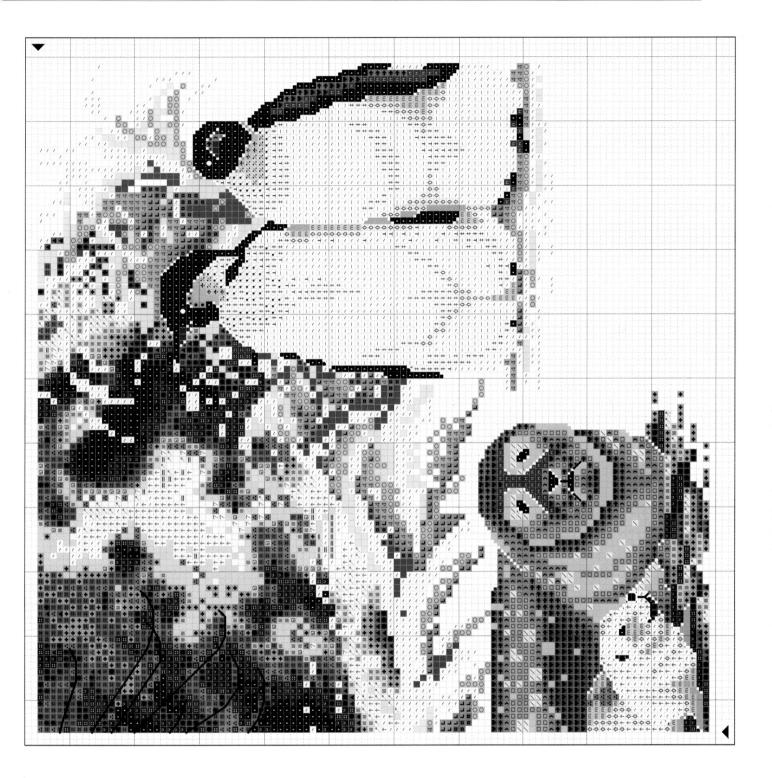

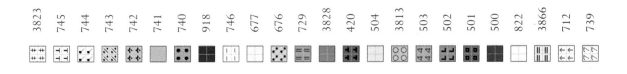

3823 745 744 743 742 741 740 918 746 677 676 729 3828 420 504 3813 503 502 501 500 822 3866 712 739

Wolf

ONE OF THE MOST GORGEOUS OF ANIMALS, the wolf is making a comeback in many regions of the world, from North America to Ethiopia. Only a few lucky people have ever come face to face with this wonderful beast, but we all know him through our pet dog, stories and legends. This head and shoulder picture, with the piercing eyes and luscious coat, is worked to perfection using subtle shading and shown most dramatically when worked on black Aida.

STITCH IT

Fabric:	*14 count black Aida 43 x 35cm (17 x 14in)*
Threads:	*DMC stranded cotton (floss) (see thread list page 113)*
Stitch count:	*150 x 106*
Design size:	*27 x 19cm (10¾ x 7½in) approx*
Stitches:	*Whole cross stitch, three-quarter cross stitch*

Prepare your fabric for work and mark the centre point (see Workbox). Follow the chart on pages 104/105, using two strands of stranded cotton (floss) for all cross stitch.

Mount and frame your picture to complete or see Display It, page 114.

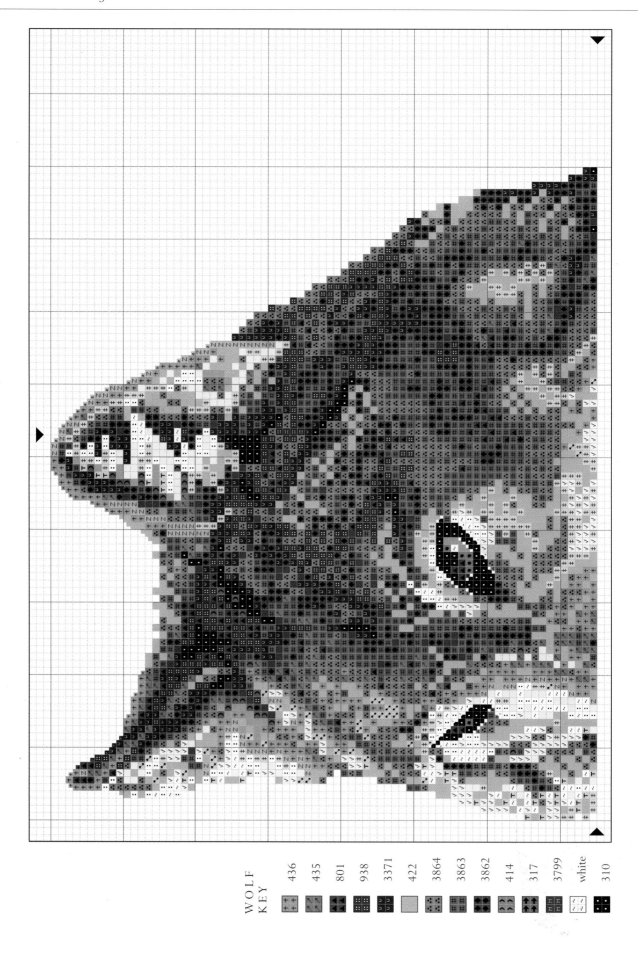

WOLF
KEY

| 436 | 435 | 801 | 938 | 3371 | 422 | 3864 | 3863 | 3862 | 414 | 317 | 3799 | white | 310 |

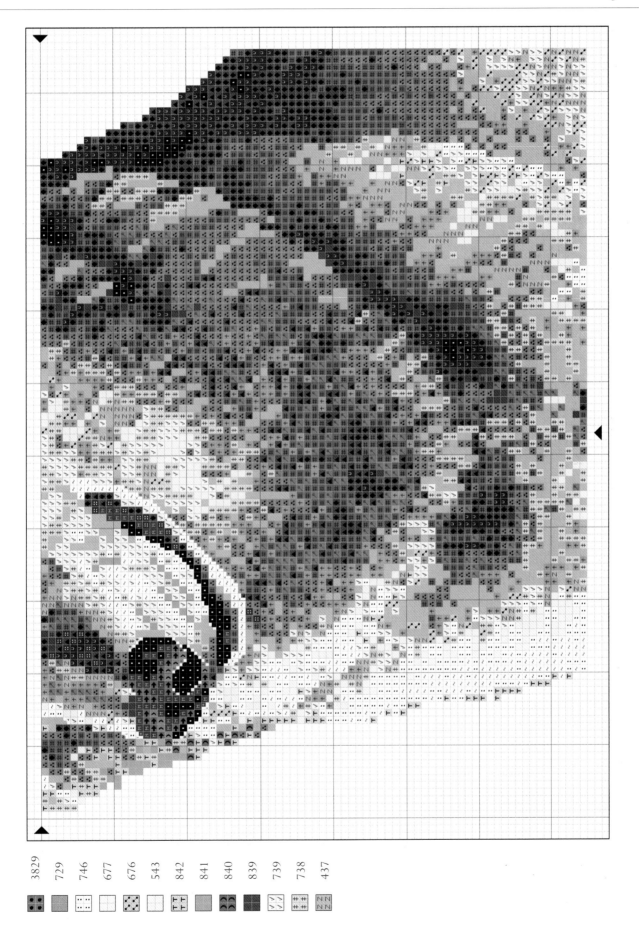

3829 729 746 677 676 543 842 841 840 839 739 738 437

Adélie Penguins

THERE ARE SEVENTEEN SPECIES of penguins.
Only six of these breed in Antarctica, and only
two of these six are exclusive to Antarctic –
the emperor penguin and the Adélie
penguin. The Adélie is the most common of
all penguins in Antarctica and for this design
I have depicted some launching themselves
from an icy ledge into the sea to feed on krill.
On land, they find walking arduous and
instead opt to toboggan, but once in the water
they are much more agile.

STITCH IT

Fabric:	*14 count sky blue Aida* *51 x 38cm (20 x 15in)*
Threads:	*DMC stranded cotton (floss)* *(see thread list page 113)*
Stitch count:	*170 x 98*
Design size:	*31 x 18cm (12 x 7in) approx*
Stitches:	*Whole cross stitch, three-quarter cross stitch, backstitch*

Prepare your fabric for work and mark the
centre point (see Workbox). Follow the chart
on pages 108/109, using two strands of
stranded cotton (floss) for all cross stitch
throughout. Work the backstitch for the eyes
with one strand of 762.

Mount and frame your picture to complete
or see Display It, page 114.

ADELIE	▦ 3768	⊍⊍ 939	ᵀᵀ 932	◆ 413	▨ 415	4 4 4 4 3033	■ 898
PENGUINS							
KEY	❖ 924	⊡ 928	❩❩ 931	ᴴᴴ 3799	⊞ 318	❭❭ 414	■ 918
	∼ white	⦂⦂ 927	▲▲ 930	⊡ 3753	❭❭ 414	⦂⦂ 3032	◥◣ 3778
	▪ 310	▦ 926	∴∴ 3750	↑↑ 3752	◆ 317	▨ 762	▨ 758

Mountain Hare

ALTHOUGH SIMILAR IN APPEARANCE to a rabbit, the hare can be distinguished by three chief points – it is bigger, has longer ears and much longer hind legs. In the winter the mountain hare's coat turns white. Unlike rabbits, they live solitary lives and never burrow. They spend their days lying in a hollow in the grass, which are known as forms, as they retain the shape of the animal's body. The young are born with their eyes open and can use their legs from birth. Each one makes its own form and is visited by the doe to be suckled. My design shows a hare just changing his coat, with a hint of a mountain range behind him.

STITCH IT

Fabric:	*14 count sky blue Aida 38 x 43cm (15 x 17in)*
Threads:	*DMC stranded cotton (floss) (see thread list page 113)*
Stitch count:	*100 x 123*
Design size:	*18 x 22cm (7 x 8¾in) approx*
Stitches:	*Whole cross stitch, three-quarter cross stitch, backstitch*

Prepare your fabric for work and mark the centre point (see Workbox). Follow the chart on page 112, using two strands of stranded cotton (floss) for all cross stitch. Work the backstitch in two strands of black 310 stranded cotton (floss) for the eye outline.

Mount and frame your picture to complete or see Display It, page 114.

869	677	644	3781	3042	3826	M O U N T A I N
801	676	642	783	3041	975	H A R E K E Y
938	422	640	781	928	469	
white	3828	3790	780	927	936	414
310	420	746	822	926	3743	413

WOLF THREAD LIST

1 skein each DMC stranded cotton (floss)

310	black	839	dk beige brown	3864	lt grey brown	746	off white
437	lt tan	414	dk silver grey	543	v. lt beige brown	801	dk coffee brown
blanc	white	840	med beige brown	422	lt hazelnut brown	729	med golden sand
738	lt tan	3862	dk grey brown	676	lt golden sand	435	lt golden brown
3799	dk pewter grey	841	lt beige brown	3371	black brown	3829	dk golden sand
739	lt tan	3863	med grey brown	677	lt golden sand	436	tan
317	silver grey	842	lt beige brown	938	dk coffee brown		

ADELIE PENGUINS THREAD LIST

1 skein each DMC stranded cotton (floss)

924	v. dk grey green	318	lt silver grey	930	dk antique blue	3778	lt terra cotta
413	dk silver grey	928	v. lt grey green	3782	lt mocha brown	3753	ultra v. lt antique blue
3768	dk grey green	415	silver grey	931	med antique blue	918	dk red copper
317	silver grey	939	v. dk navy blue	3033	v. lt mocha brown	3799	v. dk pewter grey
926	med grey green	762	v. lt pearl grey	932	lt antique blue	898	v. dk coffee brown
414	dk silver grey	3750	v. dk antique blue	758	v. lt terra cotta		
927	lt grey green	3032	med mocha brown	3752	v. lt antique blue		

2 skeins each DMC stranded cotton (floss)

310	black	blanc	white

MOUNTAIN HARE THREAD LIST

1 skein each DMC stranded cotton (floss)

310	black	926	med grey green	677	v. lt golden sand	3826	dk rust
780	ultra v. dk topaz	420	dk hazelnut brown	3743	v. lt silver plum	644	med beige grey
blanc	white	927	lt grey green	746	off white	413	dk silver grey
781	v. dk topaz	3828	hazelnut brown	936	v. dk avocado green	822	lt beige grey
938	ultra dk coffee brown	928	v. lt grey green	3790	ultra dk beige grey	414	dk silver grey
783	med topaz	422	lt hazelnut brown	469	avocado green		
801	dk coffee brown	3041	dk silver plum	640	v. dk beige grey		
3781	dk mocha brown	676	lt golden sand	975	v. dk rust		
869	v. dk hazelnut brown	3042	lt silver plum	642	dk beige grey		

DISPLAY IT

Here are just a few suggestions for displaying the animals featured in this chapter. The Polar Wildlife opening design could be stitched as a complete picture or would make a wonderful cushion (see page 124 for instructions). Each of the smaller motifs could be used on its own as a small picture. The emperor penguins could be inset into a mug or card or made up into a pincushion, using a complementary backing fabric and finishing the edges with bias binding or braid. The orca could be stitched with white beads used instead of cross stitch to emphasize the water droplets falling from the fins. Parts of the leaping penguins design could be used for a very small picture, using only the three penguins in the foreground. The wolf would look super if stitched in wool (yarn) on canvas as a wall hanging (see pages 119 and 126 for advice).